Withdrawn
from
Collection

The Young Rockhound's Handbook

The Young Rockhound's Handbook

by W. R. C. Shedenhelm

G. P. Putnam's Sons • New York

Unless otherwise indicated, illustrations are by the author and are used with the permission of Behn-Miller Publishers, Inc., and *Rock & Gem* magazine, 16001 Ventura Boulevard, Encino, California 91436.

Photo credits: Arkansas Tourist Commission, p. 72; Michigan Tourist Commission, p. 77; Oregon State Highway Travel Section, p. 24.

Copyright © 1978 by W. R. C. Shedenhelm
All rights reserved.
Published simultaneously in Canada by
Longman Canada Limited, Toronto.
Printed in the United States of America
12 up

Library of Congress Cataloging in Publication Data
Shedenhelm, WRC
    The young rockhound's handbook.
    Includes bibliographical references and index.
    SUMMARY: Explains the formation of rocks and minerals
and describes their location, characteristics,
and identification. Also explains how to polish
and cut minerals, prospect for gold, and collect specimens.
    1. Rocks—Collectors and collecting—Juvenile
literature. [1. Rocks 2. Minerals] I. Title.
QE433.S5   552'.0075   77-12632
ISBN 0-399-20624-8

Second Impression

Contents

• 1 •

Rocks Are Everywhere

One thing is certain. If you decide to collect and study rocks, you'll never run out of things to collect and study. The earth is one big mass of rock, with the thinnest imaginable film of gases and living things stuck to its outermost surface. Even the oceans, which make up very little of the total mass of the earth, are made of molten rock! And by all standard definitions of what minerals and rocks are, ice also qualifies. Many rocks are made up of oxides of various elements, and ice is an oxide of hydrogen. gen. It just so happens that ice turns to liquid, as any rock will, at a rather low temperature. Greenland, Antarctica, and the North Polar Sea are covered with ice rocks; the warmer regions are covered with molten ice, or ice lava, that we call water.

How did all this come about, this formation of the earth, of a sphere of rock very much like Mars, Venus, and Mercury that circles the star we call the sun? We don't know for certain, but we think that material left over from the creation of the sun lumped together, or coagulated, due to uneven density in the thinly spread cloud of gases and microscopic solids drifting through space. Denser areas exerted slight gravitational pulls on sparser areas, drawing material away from them. The largest clusters of material slowly swept up other matter thinly scattered around the spinning discs of gas and plasma, until the various planets were formed. Occasional smaller collections of matter formed into satellites of the larger masses. We don't know that this is exactly what happened, but from all evidence this is most probably the way the planets and our earth originated. Questions of where the gases and dust came from originally are perhaps unanswerable. The steady-state theory holds that the universe has always been, and always will be, much as it is now, with new matter and energy replacing the old from some unknown source. The big-bang theory says that it all started with an enormous primeval explosion, and that the entire universe is expanding away from the center of that original bang. A variation on this theory says that the universe may expand only so far; then it will collapse back on itself to explode again, starting the whole process over once more.

While we can only make intelligent guesses about the origin of the universe and the solar system, we are reasonably sure that our earth formed as a solid ball about 4.5 billion years ago. In all probability, it took about half a billion years for everything to cool down enough for normal geological processes such as faulting, erosion, mountain building, and the formation of sedimentary rocks to start. Through radioactive dating we can tell the age of some ancient rocks. Many of the radioactive elements found in rocks decay, or change into other elements, at exceedingly slow rates. By comparing the amount of the original radioactive element left in a rock with the amount of whatever element it has changed into, we can determine how long the radioactive element has been sealed in the rock. These elements are sealed in when the rock is last frozen into its solid state.

The oldest rock on earth that has been dated this way comes from Greenland, and is 3.8 billion years old. The Morton gneiss of southwestern Minnesota is dated at 3.6 billion years. It is almost impossible to imagine what millions of years really mean, much less billions. Here's a comparison that will give you a better idea. Let's assume that you're 20 years old and that these 20 years equal the 4 billion years it took things on earth to settle down geologically. Okay. Those earliest rocks from Greenland were formed when you were one year old, the gneiss in Minnesota when you were two. There might have been some simple, one-celled organisms in the seas by the time you were four, but we don't have evidence of life in the rocks of North America until you were ten and a half. Complex life, leaving definite fossil remains, didn't start until the end of the Precambrian, when you were seventeen, only three years ago. That's why that old saying, "When the world was new, and life began," is not at all accurate.

It was only a year and a half ago that the immense forests whose fossils make up the vast coal beds of most of the world came into being. A few months after that dinosaurs evolved, and ruled the earth for 150 million years, or about 9 months. The first identifiable man appeared in Africa 3 days ago. Egyptian and Sumerian civilizations blossomed 12 minutes ago. Christ was born 5 minutes ago. The Colonies became the United States of America

30 seconds ago, and your life of 20 years flitted by in the last 3 seconds. There's your comparison: 20 years reduced to 3 seconds.

The chemical elements that make up the earth combine with various other elements to form the molecules of slightly more complex materials. While there can be a wide variety of combinations of elements, there is a limited number of these combinations. The atoms and molecules usually arrange themselves into neat and orderly planes, or grids, so that the physical properties of the material are always very similar. Usually they are placed so that we can see and measure them. Halite—common table salt—and iron pyrite tend to form perfect cubes. Calcite and gypsum tend to form lopsided, flattened cubes—rhombohedrons. Ice is often a six-sided crystal, as can be seen in snowflakes. Scientists who study minerals—mineralogists and crystallographers—have already identified approximately twenty-five hundred distinct mineral species, and the end is not in sight. Often the differences are very small, perhaps a single additional atom in a molecule made up of several dozen atoms.

Some of these minerals often occur in small amounts, but many of them are quite common and abundant. Combined with other minerals—or alone if there is enough of any one of them—these minerals make up what we call rocks. The quartz minerals and the feldspars alone make up most of the surface of the earth. Throw in ice as a rock, and you've added quite a bit more.

We rockhounds are basically amateur geologists and amateur mineralogists, plus a dash of amateur crystallographer. We are fascinated by the great variety of forms and colors that minerals and rocks have. Professional

A common igneous rock, welling up from moderate subsurface depths, is granite. When the minerals which make up granite crystallize into an extremely coarse rock, it is known as a pegmatite.

scientists can explain why these forms and colors occur, but too often they leave out the one factor that most interests us: beauty. It's much like describing a painting by telling how the canvas was prepared and how the pigment was mixed, without ever looking at the painting as an artistic creation.

Scientists are getting an increasingly better idea of how and why minerals form. This is indeed important. Part of the current thinking has to do with the effects of plate tectonics, the recently accepted idea that the continents are being moved slowly by still-unexplained forces beneath them, deep within the earth. One plate sliding under another and plunging steeply downwards creates all sorts of interesting conditions of heat and pressure, just what is needed to create great masses of granite. This movement also releases extremely hot fluids carrying atoms and molecules that then form new mineral deposits in the less drastic physical conditions occurring nearer the surface.

The formation of mineral deposits need worry us no

more than the problem of the formation of the earth. Both are fascinating, but are only background to our private search for rocks and minerals. We searchers are called rockhounds. Many rockhounds object to this name, feeling that it is corny (which it is), but no one has come up with a better all-around name for the amateur prospector.

When you start to shape and polish rocks and minerals, you become a lapidary. Not a lapidist; there's no such word. You're a lapidary, and you do lapidary work, using lapidary tools. And, when you start cutting facets on gemstones, you are a facetor who uses a machine called a faceter. But for now, you're a rockhound.

One of the great advantages of being a rockhound is that you are automatically more aware of the earth around you than the vast majority of other people. You become more a part of the environment, and you are able to see both its unsuspected treasures and its extreme fragility. You begin to realize what the earth really is and what it means to all of us.

Perhaps the most fitting and beautiful statement on the total environment was made by Chief Seattle of the Duwamish Indian tribe. The Duwamish lived in the Puget Sound area in the state of Washington. In 1854 President Franklin Pierce offered to buy much of the Duwamish land from the tribe, promising them a safe reservation somewhere else. Here is part of what Chief Seattle said in reply.

How can you buy or sell the sky, the warmth of the land? The idea is strange to us. If we do not own the freshness of the air and the sparkle of the water, how can you buy them?

Every part of this earth is sacred to my people. Every shining pine needle, every sandy shore, every mist in the dark woods, every clearing and humming insect is holy in the memory and experience of my people. So, when the Great Chief in Washington sends word that he wishes to buy our land, he asks much of us. We will consider your offer to buy our land. But it will not be easy.

We know that the white man does not understand our ways. One portion of the land is the same to him as the next, for he is a stranger who comes in the night and takes from the land whatever he needs. The earth is not his brother, but his enemy, and when he has conquered it, he moves on. His appetite will devour the earth and leave behind only a desert.

Our ways are different from your ways. The sight of your cities pains the eyes of the red man. There is no quiet place in the white man's cities. No place to hear the unfurling of leaves in spring, or the rustle of an insect's wings. But perhaps it is because I am a savage and do not understand.

We will consider your offer to buy our land. If we decide to accept, I will make one condition: the white man must treat the beasts of this land as his brothers. I have seen a thousand rotting buffaloes on the prairie, left by the white man who shot them from a passing train. I am a savage and I do not understand how the smoking iron horse can be more important than the buffalo we kill only to stay alive. What is man without the beasts? If all the beasts were gone, man would die from a great loneliness of spirit. For whatever happens to the beasts, soon happens to man. All things are connected.

This we know: the earth does not belong to man; man belongs to the earth. Whatever befalls the earth befalls the sons of the earth. Man did not weave the web of life; he is merely a strand in it. Whatever he does to the web, he does to himself.

So wrote Chief Seattle over 120 years ago. It is time that we listened to his words.

· 2 ·

Why Some Rocks
Are Pretty

We know that chemical elements blend together to form various minerals, and that these minerals can blend together to form rocks. But why are some of these minerals —and in some cases rocks—considered pretty, even beautiful? Why are some valuable? Why are some merely called minerals, while others are gemstones or gems?

There are several basic characteristics a mineral must have to qualify as a valuable gem, and these have varied somewhat at different times and with different peoples. In almost every case, a rock or a mineral must be attractive or even striking in order to be coveted and desired. Although personal tastes differ, this would generally mean that the gemstone is distinctly and brightly colored. Transparent stones have an advantage because they can be artificially faceted to display more brilliance. True, many minerals occur in nature with facets—quartz crystals are quite common—but these are natural crystal facets, rather than man-made facets, and are not usually angled to reveal the most sparkle or fire. Here indeed is

Minerals grow into many wondrous and fascinating forms. This is a "selenite rose," a form of gypsum, which grows in wet sand.

an excellent example of how man can improve on nature.

Another important criteria for a gem, but not for a mineral, is rarity. Thus rubies and sapphires are particularly valuable because there simply aren't many of them in the earth. Gem-grade diamonds, on the other hand, are not exceedingly rare, but the supply to the world's jewelers is controlled quite rigidly by the International DeBeers Consolidated Mines, Ltd., which keeps prices both high and stable.

I should make a distinction here regarding gemstones. I have been talking about natural gemstones, which form within the earth. In the last fifty or so years, various industrial processes have been discovered and developed whereby the same chemical components that make up natural gemstones can be formed into exact, or almost exact, duplicates. These are called synthetic gemstones. In the case of many, such as the corundum gems—ruby and sapphire—fine powder is shot into an extremely hot hydrogen-oxygen flame and a small pillar, or boule, of synthetic ruby or sapphire forms. The synthetic emeralds, usually made by the Chatham process, or a derivation of it, are much closer to the borderline between synthetic and natural. They are actually grown in a "bomb" of sorts, with pressures and temperatures quite high and similar to those beneath the earth's surface where natural emeralds would form.

Both synthetic rubies and synthetic emeralds defy detection by normal means. Even a skilled and practiced gem appraiser often cannot distinguish the synthetics from natural stones without using special instruments. Many of the more sensitive lab tests will show no distinctive difference: the specific gravity (or density) is the same, the index of refraction (the amount light is bent in passing through the material) is the same, and often the reaction to ultraviolet light is the same—although this is not always so. Some natural stones will fluoresce or glow under ultraviolet light, often with a characteristic color. Some synthetics do, too. But some of both the naturals and synthetics don't. Thus, the results of ultraviolet testing are often inconclusive.

Under a microscope we begin to pick up some differences between natural and synthetic gemstones. The synthetics formed as high-temperature boules are completed quite rapidly—in a matter of minutes or hours. The layers of molten material do tend to accumulate in the basic crystal pattern of the mineral, but they develop too rapidly to allow for really neat and precise corners between surfaces or crystal faces. To examine a suspected synthetic through a mineralogical microscope, you would search within the stone for an area where crystal faces meet. In a natural stone, which takes many years to form, these angles or corners are extremely sharp and well-defined. In synthetics, stones cut from boules, the angles are rounded, even sloppy.

I'm still evading the problem of the role rarity plays in determining the value of gemstones, but let me present the case of synthetic emeralds. As I mentioned, these are grown slowly in pressure bombs, simulating the way they form within the earth. Here the molecules have more time to deposit into a precise crystal matrix, to form neatly stacked layers as they do in nature. Thus the crystal surfaces are clearer, and the corners or angles between the layers within the crystal are nearly perfect. Synthetic emeralds are often all but impossible to distinguish from natural emeralds. The reason is obvious: they practically *are* natural. The color can be anything the crystal grower wants, or the customer orders. By increasing or decreasing the key trace elements that produce the green color, the final product can be a light or a deep green. This is important if the buyer is trying to add to or replace a stone in a Russian or Brazilian necklace and wants a perfect match.

The only detectable difference then between the synthetic and natural emeralds is that nature isn't as perfect as the laboratory. Natural emeralds weighing over a few carats are seldom without very small flaws. Often they are noticeable only under the 10-power hand lens, or loupe, used by jewelers, but such flaws almost always occur in natural emeralds. So, if the expert looks at a small emerald and finds it flawless, it can be either natural or synthetic. A larger stone without flaws is probably synthetic.

Many other less valuable gemstones are synthesized these days, most by the high-temperature Linde process or variations of it. Much of the production is not for jewelry, but for watch and motor bearings, laser pumps (some of the earliest lasers were ruby lasers), and such.

But, to get back to that quality of a mineral most important in making it a gem—rarity. If a synthetic gemstone is an exact duplicate in almost every respect—composition, color, hardness, brilliance, sparkle, what have you—should it be any less valuable or desirable than a natural stone? Many people claim that the difference is unimportant and that as long as both are of equal beauty, both should be of equal value. Yet price a natural ruby and a synthetic one and you will find a vast difference. Perhaps this will change as people appreciate beauty more and rarity less.

In passing I will mention a third category of gemstones, those called artificial or imitation. These are the out-and-out fakes, which have only a superficial relationship to true gemstones—their appearance. Colored glass may look like a ruby or an emerald from a distance, but at closer range it wouldn't fool an expert for a second, and usually wouldn't fool a nonexpert for much longer. Imitations rarely have the right "look." They lack a certain richness, sparkle, or fire. They may be extremely colorful, but they just don't look valuable. There are many awfully good fakes around, to be sure, but these days they are more apt to be synthetics than imitations.

Another factor in judging the desirability of gemstones has been of particular importance in the more mobile societies of eastern Europe and the Middle East. How do you keep your wealth if you know you may have to flee the country at a moment's notice? Local currency wouldn't do you any good in another country, and it's apt to be bulky—two suitcases full of paper money won't do. How about gold? Too heavy. It's not easy to slip by customs and border officials with a two-hundred-pound briefcase without looking a little suspicious. But gems and jewels—even a hundred thousand dollars worth of diamonds, rubies, emeralds, and sapphires could be easily concealed. So, an important quality of gemstones that is often overlooked is portability.

To discover another desirable quality that a gemstone should have, glance over the listing below and notice the position of the various gem materials.

Hardness of Facetable Gem Materials

MOHS HARDNESS SCALE

Diamond	10	Cairngorm	7
Corundum	9	Citrine	7
Ruby	9	Peridot (olivine)	6.5-7
Sapphire	9	Kornerupine	6.5
Chrysoberyl	8.5	Titania (synthetic)	6.5
Spinel	8	Garnet (andradite)	6.5
Topaz	8	Cassiterite	6-7
Beryl	7.5-8	Epidote	6-7
Aquamarine	7.5-8	Spodumene	6-7
Emerald	7.5-8	Kunzite	6-7
Goshenite	7.5-8	Benitoite	6-6.5
Heliodor	7.5-8	Feldspar	6-6.5
Morganite	7.5-8	Adularia	6-6.5
Garnet		Sanidine	6-6.5
Almandite	7.5	Prehnite	6-6.5
Grossularite	7	Zircon (noncrystalline)	6-6.5
Pyrope	7	Opal	5.5-6.5
Rhodolite	7	Beryllonite	5.5-6
Spessartite	7.5	Brazilianite	5.5
Uvarovite	7.5	Obsidian	5.5
Andalusite	7-7.5	Scapolite	5-6
Iolite	7-7.5	Apatite	5
Tourmaline	7-7.5	Fluorite	4
Quartz		Sphalerite	3.5
Amethyst	7		

Okay, got it? The Mohs Hardness Scale is a comparative one, wherein a higher rating is always harder, but not in any direct or specific amount. That is, topaz at Mohs Scale 8 might be twice as hard as quartz at Mohs Scale 7, but diamond at 10 isn't simply twice as hard as corundum at 9; it's 30 or 40 times harder! Now the important thing to notice in the list of facetable gem materials is that all of the really valuable ones are much harder than quartz, at Mohs Scale 7, with most of the semi-precious gemstones quite near quartz in hardness. The reason is obvious, once you stop to think about it. Most of the earth's crust is silicon dioxide—quartz in one form or another: dust, sand, granite, sandstone. If we facet a gemstone to reveal all its hidden depths of beauty, then subject it to rubbing against our body and clothes— with their fine coating of natural quartz dust—we would quickly wear the sharp edges off the facets if the gems weren't harder than quartz. This also explains why the gem materials near quartz in hardness, or softer, are more often cut in smoothly rounded cabochons rather than being faceted. The slight wear doesn't show up as markedly on a smoothly rounded face as on a flat facet or a sharp facet edge.

MOHS SCALE OF HARDNESS*

1 Talc	6 Orthoclase
2 Gypsum	7 Quartz
3 Calcite	8 Topaz
4 Fluorite	9 Corundum
5 Apatite	10 Diamond

* You will quite frequently see the Mohs Scale misspelled as the Moh's Scale. The originator's name was Fred Mohs, not Moe or Moh. The correct spelling then can only be the Mohs or the Mohs' Scale.

Another relatively important characteristic that a mineral should have to qualify as an ideal gemstone is toughness. This is not the same as hardness. Hardness is the ability of one substance to scratch or abrade another; toughness is the ability to hold together without breaking, fracturing, cleaving, or shattering. Diamond certainly is the hardest gem material, but it's not really very tough. That is why you see pictures of diamond cutters going through such anguish when they cleave a large, rough diamond into more easily faceted pieces. A diamond will cleave, or break smoothly, along several definite planes within its crystalline form. The diamond cutter studies the rough crystal for days, weeks, even months, trying to determine in exactly which directions these planes of comparative weakness lie. If he is correct, a light tap with a hammer on a thin blade is enough to split the rough diamond into two neat parts. If he goofs, he may end up with a handful of almost worthless fragments.

Here is an example of the other side of the coin: jade is not particularly hard, which is why it is relatively easy to carve and polish. But it is extremely tough, which explains why lacy and seemingly frail jade carvings can be made.

So far in this chapter we have been talking mostly about why some minerals are valuable and less about why they are pretty. We have said that a stone's prettiness or beauty is important, that rarity helps, that portability can be important, and that hardness and toughness are assets. But how about the everyday rocks and minerals that you and I are apt to find and collect? For our purposes we can pretty well rule out all the qualities noted except beauty. Rarity only comes into mineral collecting with the rich and advanced collector, as a form of snobbishness. Portability? If you're going to start a rock and mineral collection, forget portability. Your room, your garage, and probably half the backyard will be piled with specimens. Hardness and toughness? Not really of any great importance unless you plan to use the minerals for jewelry. The only major problem with some of the more fragile mineral specimens is in keeping them out of the hands of your unknowing family and friends. Their heartfelt apologies won't put back together a shattered specimen.

Probably the most attractive minerals are those with the brightest and most distinct colors. Next in importance, generally, are the minerals which occur in large and neatly formed crystals. People are always amazed that nature can produce perfect crystals. "Why, they look almost man-made!" Of course they do—that's what facetors are imitating.

The colors themselves are due to small amounts of various elements, often the metallic elements. The blue color of turquoise comes from an extremely small amount of copper. It's so small, in fact, that turquoise is not technically considered a copper mineral.

These trace elements can make amazing differences in color, too. The red ruby and the blue sapphire would seem to have little in common. Yet both are almost identical variations of the mineral corundum. If it weren't for the differences in color, it's very likely that no one would have noticed the extremely slight difference in composition. Beryl is another example. This mineral, again with fantastically slight chemical differences, occurs as light blue aquamarine, yellow morganite, and green emerald.

When we get into mineral identification in Chapter 8,

Agate nodules, with their ugly exteriors, are often extremely beautiful when cut open, or cut into thin slabs, as shown here.

we'll get a little more into which elements cause some of the coloration, but this information is really not of too great importance. It's sort of nice to know, but not vital, unless of course you want to be a crystallographer. About the only thing most graduate geologists remember about the source of colors in minerals is that if you're asked why a particular rock or mineral is reddish, you can say it's due to iron, and you'll be right 80 percent of the time. If the mineral in a rock is white-to-pinkish, you can say that it's a feldspar, and you'll be right about as often. Naturally, these are generalizations, but they can save a lot of time.

There are many technical reasons why rocks and minerals are pretty, but they need not concern us too much. There's the old cliché: "I don't know much about art, but I know what I like." We can say the same: "I don't know much about crystallography, inorganic chemistry, or solid-state physics, but that sure is a pretty piece of rock!" And why not? We don't have to understand all the geological forces that formed a mountain range to appreciate the beauty of the Sierra Nevada, the Rockies, or the Appalachians. True, it may add a fillip to that appreciation, but it's far from required. The same holds for rocks and minerals. Collect the ones that appeal to you, that you find pretty.

If you want to know more about the rocks and minerals you collect, read some of the mineral identification books listed in Chapter 9 or see if your local high school's evening courses (or those of your local college) offer courses in mineral identification. There is an excellent home study course in mineral identification (going on into gems and jewelry) given by the Gemological Institute of America, 1660 Stewart Street, Santa Monica, California 90406. Write for its free brochure on mineral identification.

· 3 ·

Starting Your Rock and Mineral Collection

You probably already have a rock collection started. If you are interested enough in rocks and minerals to read this book, you very likely have a few specimens that you picked up in your travels. One rock does not make a collection, but more than one does. Now that you are about to become a serious collector, or even a not so serious collector, you can start referring to rocks as specimens. That's all it takes. You're on your way!

While many collections are simply a mishmash of odds and ends, picked up locally or on trips, collectors generally assign a basic subject or theme to their collections. You could try to collect one example of every recognized mineral species, but they number somewhere around twenty-five hundred, so that idea can be ruled out.

An easier theme, and a very interesting one, is the rocks and minerals of your county or state. It's amazing how many people are ignorant of the wonders that surround them, be they mineral, animal, or vegetable. You

The minerals that are the most fun to have in your collection are those you gather yourself. Anyplace where rocks are exposed is a possibility: quarries, road cuts, stream banks, hillsides. Here two rockhounds search for calcite crystals in an abandoned limestone quarry in California.

It is usually easier to clean up mineral specimens at home, rather than in the field, and this can be done with a few simple tools. Often those that looked good in the field are duds, while the "funny looking rocks" turn out to be beauties.

could visit collecting locations in your area which are listed in the regional guides (see Chapter 9). Check with local rockhound clubs. Write to your state's mineral information source (again, see Chapter 9). Local rock shops very often sell local specimens. Stop at any road cuts or excavations. All you need is a geology pick and some paper bags for your specimens. A carpenter's hammer will do in a pinch. In some places even a countywide collection could grow unmanageably huge; in others you'd have to scrape to come up with half a dozen specimens.

Depending on your location and interests, you could specialize in a particular mineral family: quartz minerals, copper minerals, iron pyrites, or garnets from the Manhattan schist—the "basement rock" under much of New York's Manhattan Island. Even a collection of fire opal from famous opal fields around the world could be started with relatively inexpensive, small samples of each. Some could be gathered personally if you had the time and resources; others could be bought at gem shows and through the mail from California, Nevada, Idaho, central Mexico, and the Australian outback.

If you are swapping or buying minerals through the mail (there is a list of dealers in Chapter 9), you could specialize in a foreign country, or a particular place. Your chances of getting a specimen of every species are about as remote as your chances of collecting every postage stamp ever issued, but that shouldn't spoil the fun.

Accumulating a representative collection of a country's minerals can be as easy or as difficult as you wish, depending on the country you select. To call a collection representative is a sly way of saying that it really doesn't contain as many examples of the area's minerals as it should. Only your budget would limit the size of your representative collection in such countries as the United States, Mexico, Brazil, Peru, Australia, and India. Or, if you like challenges, take the opposite tack and try to establish a good collection from Tibet or Nepal (I saw a few Nepalese minerals at the 1977 Tucson show). Huge quantities of excellent minerals are coming from southwest Africa, but whom do you know who has a collection of minerals from Egypt or Afghanistan?

If you are interested in or connected with the fields of automobiles, construction, or electronics, you could collect the minerals that supply the basic material for these industries. How many of the components in an automobile come from the earth? Iron, aluminum, and copper certainly. Silica for the glass. Tungsten, carbon, and molybdenum quite likely. Kaolin clays for spark plug insulators.

A small but select collection, probably made up of gemstones rather than common minerals, could be focused on minerals with historic or legendary significance. Read Dashiell Hammett's *The Maltese Falcon*; find out what jewels the Knights of Malta would have used to stud the golden bird; then accumulate the gems and create your own Maltese Falcon!

The Bible tells of the breastplate of Aaron and its twelve precious stones. Over the centuries some of the mineral names have changed, or they have been lost in cross translations, but modern experts believe that the twelve stones were: carnelian, peridot, emerald, garnet, lapis lazuli, rock crystal (quartz), zircon, agate, amethyst, citrine, onyx, and jasper. Try collecting these or the twelve foundation stones of ancient Jerusalem: sardius (carnelian), chrysolite, beryl, jasper, sapphire, chalcedony, emerald, sardonyx, amethyst, hyacinth, chrysoprase, and topaz—each represents a particular gate, tribe, and apostle. The difficulty of completing your collection of either of these sets could be increased if you insist that the stones come from the original sources (or as close to them as possible today), or that you yourself find all of them within the United States, Yes, even the emeralds.

Or you might want to collect the currently recognized birthstones, as established by a jewelers' convention in 1912. Starting with January they are: garnet, amethyst, bloodstone, diamond, emerald, pearl, ruby, sardonyx, sapphire, opal, topaz, and turquoise. Where could you find diamonds? In many states, particularly in Arkansas. Rubies? North Carolina has some. Where to look for opal? Idaho, Nevada, and California. And what about pearls? Hawaii is the place to find them. You could collect all the birthstones yourself, but you would need scuba gear to fetch the pearls.

To make birthstone collecting even easier, G. F. Kunz came up with a patriotic birthstone list earlier in this century. Again, starting with January the stones are: rhodolite garnet, amethyst, californite, sapphire, green tourmaline, moss agate, turquoise, golden beryl, kunzite, aquamarine, topaz, and rubellite. Kunz's list was based on mineral collecting in the eastern states, where everything can still be found. You might also want to collect kunzite from southern California, turquoise from Nevada or Arizona, and topaz and aquamarine from Colorado.

There are literally dozens of books on the market today to help your understanding of minerals, their occurrence, and their value. Expensive coffee-table books are filled with beautiful color photographs of the best mineral specimens in the world's best collections. These are dream books, and do not have a great deal of practical information for rockhounds. The basic books, like this one, touch lightly but with a wide scope over the many facets of geology, mineralogy, crystallography, and lapidary. These books, hopefully, lead the reader on to more specialized books on minerals and collecting. Beyond that, there are college texts and technical reference books. Magazines also cover a wide range of levels, from the amateur rockhound and lapidary articles in *Rock &*

Volcanic rock (above) is often filled with cavities caused by bubbles of gases trapped in the quickly solidifying lava. If mineral-rich ground waters later circulate through such rocks, the cavities may fill with interesting minerals: agate, jasp-agate, opal, zeolites. The batch of agate (below) clearly shows the shapes of the cavities in which it was deposited, and is suitable both for small cabochons and for tumbling.

Gem, through the more complex mineralogy and crystallography of *Mineral Record*, to the highly specialized publications of mineralogical and crystallogical societies here and abroad. You can read as far as yóur interests lead you!

When the novice collector is faced with choosing from the seemingly endless list of reference books and magazines, and familiarizing himself or herself with roughly twenty-five hundred recognized mineral species, he or she is liable to throw up their hands in horror. "I'll never be able to remember all those minerals!" Of course not. No one expects you to, nor do they expect a graduate geologist to be able to do so. They don't even expect Paul Desautels, curator of minerals at the Smithsonian Institution, to remember all of them. As I've explained more thoroughly in Chapter 8, if you can recognize sixty common minerals, you've got the problem licked in at least 90 percent of the cases. Without fail, someone will hand you a dull black rock and demand that you identify it. It's embarrassing when you can't, of course, but rest assured that most mineralogists and museum curators run into the same problem. Naturally, they can identify many more minerals and rocks than your sixty, but there are a great number of specimens that can only be identified through laboratory study: chemical analysis, X-ray diffraction, and electronic microscope probes.

However, familiarity breeds competence. Once your interest in minerals has been aroused, take advantage of every opportunity to look at mineral collections. In Chapter 9 you'll find a list of the major mineral museums in the United States. Visit as many as you can. Gem and mineral shows offer an excellent opportunity to see minerals that are currently available. Too often museums are filled with ancient specimens from sites where gems haven't been found for the past hundred years. Great, but not very useful to you as a collector.

The two best sources of dates and locations for gem shows are *Rock & Gem* magazine and the *Lapidary Journal*. Both list many hundreds of shows each year, with information supplied by the sponsoring clubs or organizations. But don't make a long trip to a listed show without writing the show sponsors. Dates and locations may be changed at the last minute.

These shows offer an excellent opportunity for you to display your own collection when it has been built up to an interesting level—once it is representative, as we say. To request an entry blank you can write to the show chairman at the address shown in the listings of the magazines. Some shows are only for sponsoring club members to exhibit their collections. Others welcome outside collections. Some will supply display cases; for others you must supply your own. Some offer competitive judging, with trophies or ribbons; others are strictly noncompetitive displays. Make up your exhibit and take your chances. My *Rock & Gem* magazine display, "Minerals of Baja and Mainland Mexico," has been welcomed and snubbed, rewarded and criticized, but generally I've felt that exhibiting was well worth the travel and the work needed to set up an interesting and colorful display at half a dozen western shows each year. True, there are certain shows I'll never go back to, but this is par for the course. The vast majority are great fun, and the volunteers running the action are kindly and sincere, if not always quite on top of show business.

If you can't find a local rock club, your best bet is to write to the secretary of your region's section of the

American Federation of Mineralogical Societies. Not all rock and mineral clubs in this country are members of the Federation, but a great many of them are. Here are the names and addresses of the current secretaries:

California Federation—Jeanne Mager, 13245 Rhoda Drive, Los Altos Hills, California 94022.

Eastern Federation—Dorothy McCarthy, 6225 Springhill Court, Greenbelt, Maryland 20770.

Midwest Federation—Jean Reynolds, 107 Tuttle Avenue, Clarendon Hills, Illinois 60514.

Northwest Federation—Helen Swearingen, P.O. Box 74, Port Townsend, Washington 98368.

Rocky Mountain Federation—Verna Z. Parshall, 2620 S. Pearl Street, Denver, Colorado 80210.

South Central Federation—Anita Shier, 6315 Vanderbilt, Houston, Texas 77005.

If this doesn't work, you can write to the secretary of the overall American Federation, Dr. E. T. Rees, 806 El Monte, Twin Falls, Idaho 83301.

If there simply isn't a rockhound club near you, start your own. It's no more complicated than forming any other type of club. There are books in the public library that will help you and tell you about Robert's Rules for conducting meetings. Or throw out the books and just form a club of fellow rockhounds. The object is to share the pleasures of rockhounding and lapidary work, not to play with parliamentary procedure.

The easiest way to start a collection is to buy a commercial set of mounted mineral specimens. These are often sold in tourist shops and at gem and hobby shows. Depending on the size of the specimens and, of course, on the number of specimens, these sets can cost anywhere from about a dollar to several hundred dollars. A good mail order source is Earth Science Materials, 1900 E. Lincoln, Box 212, Fort Collins, Colorado 80522. Write for a brochure.

The important thing is to observe as many rocks and minerals as you can. Merely glancing at them is not enough; observe them carefully and all sorts of valuable information about the different rocks and minerals will slip quietly into your memory.

Gem shows are an excellent source of mineral specimens. Buying your specimens is called "silver picking." This is an outdoor "tailgating" show.

· 4 ·

Tumbling for Jewelry

After you have been collecting minerals in the field for a while, or "silver-picking" them at shows or through the mail, you will have run across many specimens which are ideal for jewelry—and, often, quite easy-to-make jewelry. You can readily create the perfect presents for your family and friends. A pretty rock you have personally collected is usually an appreciated gift, but it wears thin after a while. How many pretty rocks can a noncollector use? But a necklace, or a dangle bracelet, or a bola tie— these are different, both because you did more work to produce them, and because they can be worn.

Most crystalline mineral specimens, the delight of the mineral collector, are of little use for making the type of jewelry we are considering. Your mineral collection is safe, at least for a while. The ideal minerals, or rocks, for our purposes are those that are "cryptocrystalline"—actually crystalline, but almost imperceptibly so, and those that are amorphous—exhibiting no crystalline structure

Apache Tears (above) are small nodules of obsidian—volcanic glass—that have weathered out of large obsidian flow. Four weeks of tumbling, with increasingly finer abrasives and finally polishing powder, produced the batch of sparkling Apache Tears (below) ready to be used in a wide variety of unusual jewelry.

at all. Examples of cryptocrystalline minerals are agate, jasper, jasp-agate, turquoise, petrified wood, and opal. The most common amorphous mineral you're likely to encounter is obsidian—volcanic glass.

Many of these minerals are reasonably attractive in their rough state, but the great majority only show their true colors when they are polished. This is why the stones found lying on the beach are so pretty at first, but turn dull once you get them home and they've dried out. The wetness gives the same effect as a high polish. The layer of water smoothes over minor roughness and lets the beauty show through. Actually, the surge of the waves and the abrasiveness of the sand have done a perfectly good tumbling job on these stones. The job just hasn't been carried far enough; the abrasives haven't been fine enough to polish the rocks to a mirror surface. This is where the modern motor-powered tumbler comes in.

If you send for the catalogs of the lapidary equipment manufacturers or the jewelry supplies listed in Chapter 9, you can get a pretty good idea of the range of tumblers available on the market today. If you have a chance, visit a rock shop or mineral show so that you can see some tumblers yourself. Basically, a tumbler is a simple machine. It is driven by an electric motor which causes a closed cylinder or barrel to rotate about twenty times per minute. When filled halfway or two-thirds with rock fragments, water, and an abrasive, it will tumble this mixture twenty-four hours a day to smooth the rough edges and surfaces of the rocks until they are pleasingly rounded and shiny.

Tumbler barrels come in a variety of sizes, based on the capacity in pounds of average-weight rocks. The smallest on the market holds one and a half pounds— about the capacity of a teacup. This is an adequate size for a novice, and will cost about fifteen dollars. Many of these smaller machines are sold with enough abrasives for several batches of rocks. Complete instructions are almost always enclosed.

Larger-sized barrels, which usually need larger-sized rotating machines, come with barrels that hold 6, 12, and 24 pounds, or capacities close to these. A 6-pounder is also a good size for a beginner, but the larger barrels are often difficult to fill with rocks collected during only one field trip. They are handiest for those minerals which usually produce a high percentage of unsatisfactory results. Obsidian is a good example. Its non-crystalline amorphous state and its inherent stresses, strains, and unevenness make it particularly subject to shattering, spalling, and chipping. To make up for a poor crop, I frequently load up a 12-pound barrel with assorted pieces of obsidian and let the mineral grind with the coarse abrasive for a week or two. Then, I wash the tumbler barrel out and hand-pick through the first-stage results. The defective pieces are put aside for another tumbler run. The smoothly rounded obsidian, nearly flawless, go into a 6-pound barrel for the medium-grit stage. These may break up at this time, but after a week or so of tumbling, I inspect the batch again and take enough of the best-looking stones to fill the 1½-pound barrel three-quarters full. The final result will be my highest-grade material for jewelry or display.

Most minerals you are likely to tumble—agates and jasp-agates—do not require such a drastic process of elimination. In most cases, either a 1½-pound or 6-pound tumbler will work just fine from beginning to end.

The two most popular sizes of home tumblers are the little 1½ - pound capacity and the medium-sized 6 pound capacity. Both are motor-driven, use little electricity, and will polish a batch of rocks in about a month, running 24 hours a day.

As I mentioned, many of these smaller models come with a set of three or four grit sizes of abrasives and polish. The abrasive grits are all silicon dioxide, a very hard substance, and basically vary only in grain size. In many of the tumbler abrasive kits you can buy, the grits will simply be called coarse, medium, and fine. A four-can kit might include prepolish after fine. The final polish is generally aluminum oxide, although it may be one of several other metallic oxides used in lapidary work.

If you buy your abrasives separately (or in bulk as you will after you have done a bit of tumbling), coarse is in the 80-100 grit size range, medium is 220-400, fine is 600-800, and the occasional prepolish is 800-1200. If you plan to do much tumbling you will find that buying by the pound is less expensive than buying smaller amounts, and that buying unsorted is even cheaper. Unsorted costs less because it is easier for the manufacturer of abrasives to bag abrasives with a range of say 250–400 than to bag either 250 or 400. For the majority of tumbling purposes, buying unsorted won't make any difference. You just want a grain size somewhere between coarse and medium. So, for both coarse and medium abrasives, check the prices on these mixed sizes in 1- to 5-pound quantities. In fine abrasives, it's better to stick to the specific grit size you want, and usually this means 600.

But, when you get your tumbler, before you do anything else, read the manufacturer's instructions. Usually they are fairly complete and full of valuable information. Keep track of what you're doing on a clipboard. All you need to note is what rocks you are tumbling, what grit size you are using, and the date you started the current batch. These facts are too easy to forget after a few days or a week have gone by. I often have four or five barrels going at one time, each with different minerals, and each started at different times. I'd be lost without a program; a key number painted on the top and bottom of each barrel also helps keep things straight.

How long does tumbling take? Seemingly forever. It demands great patience, but, looking on the bright side, there is very, very little work involved. Once you charge up a barrel and send it spinning, you have almost nothing to do for at least five days, more often a week. Check the time schedule recommended by the manufacturer. I generally plan out stages for a week so that cleanups and grit changes come on Saturdays or Sundays. Depending on the hardness and toughness of the rock or mineral, the coarse stage will last a week—or sometimes two—with a refreshment of the grits. The medium and fine stage each take about a week, as does polishing. So a tumbler of average stones, say agate, will take a month—assuming the tumbler is going twenty-four hours a day, seven days a week.

Is there any way to speed up the process? Well, yes and no. The amount of necessary abrading and polishing requires a certain amount of rubbing together within the tumbler. A faster tumbler speed would only create enough centrifugal force to hold the rocks against the inner side of the tumbler barrel—there wouldn't be any tumbling action. There are several vibrating tumblers on the market that claim to cut tumbling time by a third to a half using oscillatory motion rather than rotary tumbling. I have had indifferent results with them, yet fellow rockhounds claim that if you follow the manufacturer's instructions *exactly*—which I didn't do; I ad-libbed a little—the results are as fine as anything produced by a slower rotary tumbler. The major reason vibrating tumblers are not more widely used is that they are two to three times as expensive as the same capacity rotary tumbler. So if you have the money and are in a hurry, you might try a vibrating tumbler.

Another way to speed up the production of finished baroques (irregularly shaped stones) is to start with pretumbled rocks. As far as I know these are not for sale, but the shoreline of oceans and lakes are loaded with them, free for the picking. These nicely rounded beach stones have been tumbled by the water and sand and are usually in what we would consider the coarse stage. All you have to do is see that you use a wide variety of sizes. For better tumbling action, put in medium or fine abrasive and let the tumbler run for a week. After another week of polishing you should have a beautiful collection of rounded and polished rocks, if, of course, the rocks were colorful at the outset. A rounded hunk of brick is still going to end up as a rounded hunk of brick. Maybe a little smoother, but not prettier.

Following the tumbler manufacturer's guidebook on grit sizes and length of runs with each grit, you will finally get to the polishing stage. In preparation for this, as for every grit change along the way, utmost cleanliness is essential. A single piece of coarser grit left in the tumbler barrel could scratch a lot of nicely polished rock. You should never flush used grits down the drain. They are heavy particles, and will clog up the plumbing. It is best to empty the tumbler into a sieve or colander over a plastic bucket. Hose off the rocks over the bucket first, then give them a thorough hosing over the lawn, making

Coarse, medium, and fine silicon carbide abrasives are used in the tumbler, and finally an extremely fine polishing powder. For some stones, such as obsidian, it is best to thicken the water by adding Karo to produce slower tumbling action.

certain that every last piece of grit is washed away. Then hose down the inside and outside of the tumbler barrel and lid. For drying, use paper towels that can be thrown away, so that no bits of grit are carried on to a finer stage. If you are working with several barrels at the same time, clean up the finest grit batches first so that if there is any chance of cross-pollution, it will be in the direction of getting finer particles into the coarser ones, which won't do any harm.

The polishing powder that comes with prepackaged tumbling abrasive kits is usually aluminum oxide. The majority of the other polishes available on the market are also metallic oxides of one type or another. Tin oxide and cerium oxide are highly favored, but they are quite expensive. They may not be all that much better for general tumbling use, although they may give a better polish to certain materials. This is something you may want to experiment with and decide for yourself.

Now we'll assume that you have run your first batch of rocks through the necessary week of tumbling, and have opened the barrel for the last time to check your treasures. If the material you put in at the beginning was quality stuff, you will have a nice batch of really startling baroques. Sort through them, admire the results of your early lapidary efforts, and put aside the ones that aren't quite up to standards. You can retumble them with a later batch.

Tumbled stones can be displayed in a jar or a bowl. They can be given away to be used as pocket pieces—unique and shiny stones to be fondled and displayed. If you check the lapidary supply catalogs, or visit rock shops or gem shows, you will see caplike attachments called bell caps. These gold- or silver-colored soft metal caps, shaped somewhat like bells, can be formed to fit onto oddly shaped stones. They have a small ring at the top. Naturally they won't grip a smooth stone, but modern epoxy adhesives, a major contribution to lapidary work, help solve this problem.

Select the stones that you want to make into a necklace, a bracelet, or dangles for a pendant. Arrange the stones according to sizes or colors to see how the completed project will look. Then, using modeling clay, foamed plastic, or sand, stand the stones up in their dangling position so that you can attach the bell caps to the top. Adhesive work, like tumbling, requires cleanliness. The top of each stone should be cleaned with alcohol or, better yet, with acetone. Both can be bought in most drugstores, but they are cheaper in the paint department of hardware or building supply stores.

Mix up a small amount of epoxy, following the instructions on the tubes. A bottle cap makes a good throw-away mixing pot, and a wide toothpick can serve as a stirrer. The epoxy and the hardener should be stirred together for at least thirty seconds; a minute is even better. Fast-hardening epoxy is easier to work with, if you work quickly. Slow-hardening epoxy does not become tacky as quickly, and everything needs to be better aligned and supported to keep the bell caps from slipping off their intended positions. But the slow-hardening epoxy makes a stronger bond, so it is preferred if it is practical to use. It's a good idea to have some of each on your workbench.

When the epoxy has hardened, you can clean up any smeared adhesive around the bell caps without too much trouble by using a knife point. A 2½-power magnifier is handy here. If your work looks reasonably neat at 2½-magnification, it will look super to the naked eye.

Now, with your tumbled stones bell-capped, put jump rings through the little loops atop the bell caps and through the loops of the pendant, bracelet, or necklace chain. These jump rings and chains are available at lapidary supply stores or through many of the catalogs listed at the back of this book—Grieger's and Zymex, for example.

Never open jump rings by spreading the split ends. This will deform the ring. The two ends of the split are moved sideways until the gap is large enough. Later they are closed with a reverse sideways bending. It is best to use two pairs of smooth-nosed jeweler's pliers. You will soon find that it is a good idea to have a variety of jump ring sizes and colors on hand as well as a variety of bell caps.

Using only a tumbler and some pliers, you are in the jewelry business! You have ideal gifts for friends and relatives, and you just might want to sell them, too. Try your own neighborhood first, then branch out to arts and crafts shows.

You have turned out something both personal and unique!

Tumbled baroques, in this case orthoclase feldspar, are imbedded in modeling clay for convenience, and bell caps are attached with epoxy glue.

• 5 •

Slabbing, Grinding, and Polishing

Tumbling is easy, and the results can be very colorful. There does come a time, however, when the hobbyist begins to feel overloaded with polished baroques. Every relative and every friend has been given gifts of bola ties, pendants, and necklaces. Local charities have been supplied with bowls of five-cent tumbled agate. Coffee cans and shoe boxes filled with tumbled stones line the garage shelves. It's time to move on to lapidary fields where one has more control over the final shape of the gem materials.

We'll go through the equipment needed in the sequence it will be used, rather than in order of its desirability or necessity. If you plan to collect most of your cutting material in the field, you will need some way to slice the large hunks into slabs measuring roughly ¼ inch. Pieces will then be cut from these smaller blanks and shaped and polished into discs and ovals called cabochons.

The most valuable piece of equipment for this slabbing work is called, not too mysteriously, a slab saw. The larger the diameter of the blade, the larger the chunks of rough material that can be cut. The maximum thickness that can be handled is always a factor of the blade's radius minus the hub's radius, which makes sense. Thus, the fourteen-inch diameter blade on my slab saw will cut material up to five and a half inches thick. The length of the cut that can be made depends on the travel of the clamp or vise which grips the material and travels past the rotating blade.

Unfortunately, a larger blade means a more expensive complete unit. This is due to the increasing size of the saw base and its lubricant tank, the more powerful electric motor, and the larger circular diamond blade itself. With very few exceptions, these days all slabbing and trimming of minerals is done with diamond saw blades. Very small industrial diamonds are embedded in the rim or outer edges of the steel blade and the extremely hard diamond wears away the comparatively softer rock or mineral. The rim of the blade is fairly smooth to the touch; indeed you can put your finger against the rotating blade without injury, although I don't recommend doing so!

A twenty-four-inch slab saw would be the ideal saw, but would cost close to a thousand dollars. I use a fourteen-inch slab saw, which costs a bit over five hundred dollars, and it handles most of the materials that I collect in the field. This last sentence is kind of misleading, since I try to only bring home material that I know will fit my saw. If I had a larger saw, I'd undoubtedly bring home larger pieces of rock.

You can get along without a slab saw by several methods. If you have a large chunk of what you feel to be worthwhile material, take it to a rock shop and have them slab it for you on their saw. They will charge you for wear and tear on the saw and for the time involved, but it is cheaper than buying your own saw.

Many dealers sell preslabbed cutting material at rock shops and at gem shows. The slabs are generally kept in plastic trays partially filled with water. A wet slab shows the depth of color and design that will show up when the rock reaches its final high polish. Buyers frequently carry a metal or plastic template, with cutouts for the size and shape of cabochons that particularly interest them. By sliding the template across the slabs, it is easy to visualize how the coloration and patterns will appear on a finished cabochon.

Occasionally a dealer will offer trimmed pieces of slab with standard-sized cabochon ovals marked on it with a felt-tip pen, but most lapidaries prefer to buy a whole slab and choose their own areas for cabbing.

While the need for a slab saw can be eliminated by purchasing precut slabs, it is still necessary to have a small trim saw. Fortunately, the trim saws are not too expensive. The most popular size has a six-inch diamond blade; including the blade and an electric motor it will cost from thirty to fifty dollars.

On an average slab, you might find three or four areas for interesting cabochons of different sizes by sliding the template around and orienting the short and long dimensions of the cab ovals in various ways. You should inscribe your final cab outlines on the surface of the slab. Pencil lines are apt to rub off; felt-tip lines are too wide. Rock shops and lapidary suppliers sell short pieces of aluminum or brass rod, which can be filed to a very sharp point. By keeping the point tight inside the template opening, you can leave a visible mark which will not rub or wash off.

When you have marked the cab shapes onto the slab, cut them apart with the trim saw. Since sawing is much faster and easier than grinding, you should trim to within one-eighth inch of the template lines. With its circular blade, a trim saw will only cut in straight lines, so it is necessary to plan a series of angle shots passing close to the curved control lines.

Now we get to what is universally referred to as the grinding and sanding equipment. Actually, it would be more accurate to call it shaping and smoothing equipment. The standard unit is a heavy-duty arbor, driven by a belt to the center of the shaft. Two grinding wheels, sanding belt drums, or a polishing disc can be mounted on the threaded ends. Variations on this theme include units where the two wheels, two drums, and polishing

Templates for various shapes of cabochons are available through lapidary supply dealers and are essential if the finished stone is to fit commercially available mountings. Here a stone in the first stage of shaping matches perfectly. Now the top has to be ground into a gentle curve, and smoothed and polished to a flawless finish.

disc are placed in a row. The multi-wheel units are un-doubtedly more convenient since you don't have to change wheels as you work your cabs through progres-sively finer stages of finishing. But, as the saying goes in motor racing, "Speed costs money, and more speed costs more money." Thus in lapidary work the saying would be, "Convenience costs money, and more convenience costs more money." It's a good idea to start out with a reason-ably simple and inexpensive two-wheel unit. After you have mastered the lapidary craft on this, you may decide to buy a more expensive unit. You can usually sell your basic unit to another beginner, particularly if you are a member of a rockhound club. Such clubs can be invalu-able for learning the basics of lapidary work.

The abrasive wheels and belts used for cabochons con-tain silicon carbide grits. For harder materials, and for gem faceting, diamond abrasives are popular and often essential. Because diamond wheels for your cabbing unit are much more expensive than silicon carbide wheels, I recommend that you begin with the relatively inexpen-sive carbide wheels. After you have worn down a couple of these—and learned your craft—you might want to switch to diamond wheels. Asking the opinions of the other lapidaries you will meet in a club can prove helpful in this case.

Normally, in shaping a cabochon, the cab blank moves up through five stages of shaping and polishing. The coarsest wheel, which does most of the removal of un-wanted stone, is usually a #100 grit. After the cab has been shaped to make a tight fit in the template hole, the top is domed into a smooth and even curve. Both these shapings take practice, and the beginner will end up with many offbeat cabs in the process of learning—that's part of the dues one pays.

It is easiest to round the outer edge of the cab, particularly of the larger cabs, by simply holding the stone in your fingers. However, this can lead to brushing the edge of the rapidly spinning wheel with one's fingers—a likely way to remove both fingernails and skin. Rubber fingertips—the type worn by secretaries and bookkeepers—will save skin and nails. If you can't buy any locally, you can send for some from The Great Western Company, 14812 Otsego Street, Sherman Oaks, California 91403. They cost a dollar for two, or two dollars for five.

The best way to get around this problem is to dop the

The standard grinding/polishing machine is a motor-driven arbor which will take coarse grinding wheels, finer abrasive cloth drums, and flat polishing discs at either end. Pressure or gravity water spray provides cooling and dust removal.

stone. The older and still widely used method requires a special dopping wax, available at rock shops and through lapidary supply dealers. It is melted over low heat until tacky, very much like sealing wax. The standard dop stick is a round wooden dowel about four inches long. It is handy to have a wide variety of diameters on hand, using thicker dowels on larger cabs. The end of the dowel is swirled in the soft wax, picking up a blob. The stone, which should be spotlessly clean and warmed, is pressed into the soft wax. When the wax cools, it grips the stone quite firmly.

The drawback to using wax is that it sometimes shatters due to vibration from a slightly uneven abrasive wheel. The stone being shaped is snapped into the metal wheel guard with the velocity of a rifle bullet. This could affect the lapidary in much the same way as a rifle bullet, too. One way to avoid using dopping wax is to attach the stone to a wooden or metal dop stick with epoxy glue. The problem here is that most epoxy will soften when exposed to heat. This is handy when you want to remove the stone from the dop stick, but it creates a problem when the stone accidentally gets too warm while being shaped and polished. For very small stones, about the only practical solution is to epoxy-dop the cab blanks onto the head of a nail.

A fairly new product on the market is the double-faced tape used to mount mirrors and tile onto walls. Every lapidary's shop should be equipped with a roll of this tape. It can be used to attach small objects to the workbench top, allowing both hands to be free for other things. This double-faced tape, used with special aluminum dop sticks now available through magazine ads and lapidary dealers, is much easier on the nerves than dopping wax.

A new technique, preferred by many lapidaries, is to use double-faced tape to hold stones to metal dop sticks. Acetone is used to assure the high level of cleanliness necessary for proper holding.

True, it sometimes lets the stone pull loose from the dop stick, but not without a fair warning. The stone pulls loose slowly and you can ease up on your pressure against the wheel. Again, as in all phases of lapidary work, cleanliness is essential. The flat of the dop stick and the back of the gemstone blank should be wiped with acetone to remove every trace of finger oil or other contaminants. Acetone can be bought relatively inexpensively at paint stores, where it is sold as lacquer thinner.

When the cabochon has been fairly well shaped on the coarse #100 wheel, move on to the finer #220 wheel. Here the smoothness of the cab's shape is improved upon, and the scratches left by the coarser grit are replaced by those of the #220. At this stage very little actual material is removed—this should have been done on the #100.

What is the best diameter for the wheels you are using on the cabbing unit? In an article on grinding wheels in

Rock & Gem magazine, John Sinkankas said that he considered an eight-inch wheel the minimum size, a ten-inch wheel better, and a twelve-inch wheel far superior to both. The larger wheels will cost more, as will the arbor needed to mount them, but you can feel reassured by the word of authority.

The next two steps do not remove very much material —essentially the scratches of coarser abrasives are replaced by increasingly finer ones. Drums of various designs hold a strip or loop of abrasive-coated cloth, usually with #400 and #600 grits. The dopped stone is rotated and swayed against the foam-padded cloth, first on the #400 cloth until all the #220 scratches are gone, then on the #600 until the #400 scratches are gone. It sounds more complicated and time consuming than it actually is. The majority of shaping time is spent on the #100 coarse wheel since this is where most of the material is removed.

Head-mounted magnifying glasses are very valuable in these finer stages of polishing. With glasses of about 2½-power, you can examine the surface of the cabochon for quite small scratches or flat spots. These will not show up when the surface is wet from the coolant water because the water fills the minor depressions. The surface must be dried with a paper towel or, more commonly, on your shirt front.

When the surface finally looks flawless under 2½-power magnification, the final gloss is added with the polishing pad. This is usually a flat, cast-aluminum disc. A layer of spongy rubber is glued to the face, then a disc of leather glued atop this. The leather is moistened with water from a plastic squirt bottle, or with a clean wet paintbrush. Then the polishing agent is applied.

There is as much controversy about choosing the best polish for different gem materials as there is about almost any other phase of lapidary work. The majority of readily available polishes are oxides—aluminum oxide, cerium oxide, and tin oxide are the most popular; tin is currently the most expensive. These can be bought in bulk as powder. The powder form is used in tumblers; when mixed with water it can be used in polishing cabs. Bruce Bars, cardboard-enclosed sticks of polish with a consistency similar to that of window putty, are a bit more expensive, but extremely convenient. The spinning polishing pad is moistened with water, then the Bruce Bar is rubbed across the surface and you're neatly set to go.

Small flat pieces of slabbed rock can be polished with regular tumbler abrasives on a sheet of plate glass. This is a fairly slow method of polishing, but flat pieces are difficult to do well on the rounded wheels of most machines.

The dopped stone is rotated and swayed against the revolving pad, and the surface is cleaned and checked with the 2½-power glasses from time to time until you have achieved the final jewel-like polish—a fitting description, for you have indeed created a jewel.

At some later date you may want to get into silversmithing—designing and making mountings for the stones you shape and polish—but silversmithing is another whole field in itself. The catalogs from lapidary and jewelry suppliers listed in Chapter 9 contain hundreds of mountings for cabochons cut to the standard millimeter dimensions used on cabochon templates. You can purchase belt buckles, bola tie slides, earrings, bracelets, chains, pendants, rings—indeed, you can buy just about anything you need to make jewelry from your cabochons and tumbled baroques. All items are sold in various metals, including sterling silver and 24-karat gold.

Now your gifts will be an even greater display of your

These are but a few of the hundreds of designs of mountings available for polished gemstones. The cast buckle will take three small tumbled baroques; the bola tie slides are made for oval-shaped cabochons.

individuality and craftsmanship than the jewelry you made with tumbled stones. And the pieces you choose to sell will bring a much higher price than your baroques. With a state retail seller's license, the mountings and findings—part of jewelry mounting—can be bought wholesale at anywhere from 15 to 60 percent below retail. The only other major factors to consider when pricing your finished jewelry are the value of the time it took you to make the cabochon and the cost of the cutting material.

Where should you sell your buckles, bolas, and beads? It depends on the product and the local market. Buckles might be sold on consignment through a men's shop, bracelets and necklaces through a women's shop. Gem shows are a poor market because many of the people there cut their own material; arts and crafts shows are excellent spots because few of the visitors do their own work. Inexpensive jewelry—say under five dollars—could even be sold door-to-door.

If the cabochons begin to pile up and you feel the need to try a craft that is even more exacting, and perhaps more rewarding, you can try faceting gemstones. A whole new unit is needed, which costs anywhere from three hundred fifty dollars to over a thousand dollars. There are at least half a dozen major manufacturers of home-faceting units. Their products can be found in the dealer catalogs listed in Chapter 9. Here again, seek the advice of experienced facetors in your rockhound club, read the brochures put out by the manufacturers, and buy the best unit you can afford.

If you combine rock collecting with silversmithing and lost-wax casting, you can create your own jewelry from beginning to end. You could say the sky's the limit!

• 6 •

Panning for Gold

Two factors have made panning for gold an important part of rockhounding. One factor is the change in U.S. laws made a few years ago which put all gold on the open market. Before that there were many restrictions on the private ownership of processed gold. Miners and prospectors were allowed to possess raw gold from placer or lode mines, but they had many problems trying to sell it. Also, the price was pegged at thirty-five dollars per troy ounce by the government. All this has changed—gold can now be sold internationally and 1000-fine gold (very pure) varies in price from about one hundred twenty to one hundred fifty dollars an ounce. With the price of gold at roughly four times its earlier value, gold mining can be quite profitable.

The other factor that affects gold panning is that more people have more time for outdoor recreation. There is a feeling in the United States that spending time in the mountains or the desert "doing nothing" is somehow sinful and wasteful—it goes against the concept of the

The only equipment you need for placering gold is a shovel and a pan. If the deposit turns out to be rich, sluice boxes and more efficient devices can be built or purchased.

American work ethic. This is nonsense, of course, but many people actually become quite unhappy when they aren't doing something. This explains, in part, the great popularity of trout fishing and, we must admit, rock collecting. If you're hunting for rocks and minerals, you are obviously "doing something"—you're not just loafing around and enjoying yourself!

Panning for gold carries this idea one step further. You are not only doing something by looking for pretty rocks, you are looking for *valuable* pretty rocks. Everyone understands that. You can even change your title from rockhound to prospector if you want. Many people will be duly impressed.

Today, groups of young people, adults, and even families often spend summer vacations panning for gold. Very few of these efforts ever reach the stage where they could be considered commercial operations—they're mostly just for fun. It's even rare that the vacationers make much of a profit from the summer's work. Still, what could be more exciting than spending a few weeks or a month outdoors, prospecting in sparkling creeks for gold, and coming home with a couple of bottles of nuggets and flakes of gold panned personally from the streams? The larger nuggets could be made into unique jewelry. The finer gold could be sold—if you can bear to part with it—but unless you ended up with quite a lot, it would be better to keep it as a souvenir and investment.

Placer gold is loose gold that has been washed down, or otherwise eroded, from gold in solid rock. Gold still in its original rock is called lode gold. As the tough and heavy gold is freed from the rock, it is carried down the canyons and valleys, mostly by the action of flowing water. Because gold is heavier than the sand and gravel it is travelling with, it tends to drop out of the lighter rock mixture whenever the velocity of the water slackens. The water flow may be slowed by the slope of the streambed lessening, natural obstructions or riffles on the floor of the creek, the inside of a bend in the stream, or many other physical variables. It's up to the prospector to try to visualize these variables by asking, "Where would I stop if I were a heavy nugget of gold?" The search for an answer might include studying parts of earlier streambeds which were left high up on the canyon wall as the stream eroded its way deeper into the canyon floor.

Here's a list of the locations in the seventeen states where placer gold has been found.

Alabama: Chilton, Clay, Cleburne, Coosa, Randolph, Talladega.

Alaska: Placer gold has been found in numerous scattered localities.

Arizona: Cochise, Mohave, Pima, Pinal, Yavapai, Yuma.

California: Amador, Butte, Calaveras, Del Norte, El Dorado, Fresno, Humboldt, Imperial, Kern, Los Angeles, Madera, Mariposa, Mono, Monterey, Nevada, Placer, Plumas, Sacramento, San Luis Obispo, Shasta, Sierra, Siskiyou, Trinity, Tuolumne, Yuba.

Colorado: Adams, Boulder, Chaffee, Clear Creek, Costilla, Eagle, Gilpin, Hinsdale, Jefferson, Lake, Mineral, Moffat, Montezuma, Park, Routt, San Juan, San Miguel, Summit.

Georgia: Barrow, Bibb, Carroll, Cherokee, Dawson, Douglas, Fannin, Forsyth, Fulton, Gilmer, Greene, Haralson, Hart, Henry, Lincoln, Lumpkin, Madison, Marion, McDuffie, Murray, Newton, Oglethorpe, Paulding, Rabun, Towns, Union, Walton, Warren, White, Wilkes.

Idaho: Ada, Adams, Bannock, Benewah, Boise, Bonneville, Camas, Cassia, Clearwater, Custer, Elmore, Idaho Falls, Latah, Lemhi, Owyhee, Power, Shoshone, Twin Falls, Valley, Washington.

Montana: Beaverhead, Broadwater, Deer Lodge, Fergus, Granite, Jefferson, Judith Basin, Lewis and Clark, Lincoln, Madison, Meagher, Mineral, Missoula, Park, Powell, Silver Bow.

Nevada: Clark, Douglas, Elko, Esmerelda, Eureka,

Humboldt, Lander, Mineral, Nye, Ormsby, Pershing, Washoe, White Pine.

New Mexico: Colfax, Grant, Lincoln, Otero, Rio Arriba, Sandoval, Santa Fe, Sierra, Taos.

North Carolina: Anson, Burke, Cabarrus, Caldwell, Catawba, Chatham, Cherokee, Clay, Cleveland, Davidson, Franklin, Gastonia, Granville, Guilford, Halifax, Henderson, Iredell, Lincoln, Macon, McDowell, Mecklenberg, Montgomery, Moore, Nash, Orange, Person, Polk, Randolph, Richmond, Rowan, Rutherford, Stanley, Union, Warren, Yadkin.

Oregon: Baker, Coos, Curry, Douglas, Grant, Jackson, Josephine, Union, Wheeler.

South Carolina: Cherokee, Chester, Chesterfield, Kershaw, Lancaster, Spartanburg, Union, York.

South Dakota: Custer, Lawrence, Pennington.

Utah: Beaver, Daggett, Garfield, Grand, Piute, Salt Lake, San Juan, Sevier, Uintah.

Virginia: Albemarle, Buckingham, Culpeper, Cumberland, Fluvanna, Goochland, Louisa, Spotsylvania, Stafford.

Washington: Chelan, Clallam, Ferry, Kittitas, Lincoln, Okanogan, Whatcome.

This list is from the U.S. Bureau of Mines Circular IC-8517, published in 1971. You will find information on how to get a copy at the end of this chapter. It is probably the best up-to-date basic book on placer gold and how to pan for it.

How much gold is there? There's no way of knowing for certain, of course, but we do know that between 1792 and 1969, 316,770,000 troy ounces of gold were mined in the United States. For our purposes it is interesting to note that about one-third of that amount (114,136,000 ounces) was placer gold and not lode gold. While it's true that most of the placer gold was produced with expensive machinery—huge dredges and the like—the original discovery was often made by a prospector with a gold pan. There have also been legendary locations like the Tin Cup Diggings near Downieville in California's Mother Lode Country, in the 1850s. Here the placer claims were only about ten feet square. Yet placer miners would bring home a tin cup full of nuggets every day—and they usually didn't even bother with the fine stuff.

You're not likely to find such a rich stream deposit these days, but there is no geological reason why you couldn't. Hardly a year goes by without someone in Mother Lode Country stumbling, often completely by accident, upon an incredibly large nugget. There is indeed still "gold in them there hills," and a little more is washed loose and sent down the slopes each year.

All placer gold comes from a lode supply. It has to erode out of some sort of source rock, where it was deposited from hot, mineral-forming solutions. If you can find that lode source, you could well have a very rich mine. But finding it is not always possible. For example, the true source of the California Mother Lode gold was never found.

The Sierra Nevada is largely the remnant of a huge mass of granite which formed at a considerable depth over 150 million years ago. The gold probably came out of the extremely hot molten granite, along with many other gaseous and fluid elements and compounds. The gold percolated up through the sedimentary rocks nearer the surface where it and the other elements and compounds solidified out. Over millions of years, a long fault zone occurred along what is now the eastern edge of the Sierra Nevada, and the huge block of granite tilted upward toward the west. What was left of the sedimentary rocks, much changed or metamorphosed, was slowly eroded off the underlying granite and into a large basin —now the Sacramento and San Joaquin valleys. The gold, almost as heavy as lead, didn't travel far from its source. But that particular source, or sources, simply doesn't exist anymore, and probably hasn't for many millions of years.

In other places the lode source may be too spread out to be profitably mined—not enough gold per ton of rock. But if placer gold is found, that's another matter! Gravity, water, and specific gravity have done the concentrating for us. The gold would be deposited in the sandbars or gravel when the gold's downstream movement was stopped by a change in water velocity—maybe a million years ago, maybe last Tuesday.

Your job as prospector is to look at a canyon and try to figure out where gold might have accumulated—recently or a long time ago. Part of your task is to determine the effects of gravity and water velocities; the rest is pure luck.

The tools that you will normally need are quite standard. To uncover and sift gravel and sand you will need a shovel, a pick, and a gold pan. Gold pans come in a variety of sizes—those of ten, twelve, and sixteen inches in diameter are the most widely used. The smaller sizes are easier to manage and are better for sampling; the larger sizes will handle more sand and gravel and are better for working in what seems to be a worthwhile area. Gold pans are sold at hardware stores in placer areas, and through some of the supply houses listed in Chapter 9.

The technique of panning for gold is difficult to write about but easy to demonstrate. If you see a pan-for-a-fee tourist business in placering country, stop by and get some instruction. It will save you a lot of time. What you are trying to do, basically, is to jiggle the sand and gravel in the gold pan so that the heavier gold nuggets and flakes will work their way to the bottom of the pan. This is done under water. From time to time you shove off the lighter material at the top of the pan, trying to keep the heavier material at the bottom. Hopefully you will end up with a crescent of black sand in the pan and, if you

A surplus military entrenching shovel works fine for prospecting, as does a geologist's pick. Gold pans can be purchased in most hardware stores in placer gold areas, and are quite inexpensive.

are lucky, there will be some specks of gold mixed in with this sand. The black sand is usually magnetite, a heavy iron oxide. You almost always find black sand where you find gold, but you don't always find gold where you find black sand. Because the magnetite is heavy, though not as heavy as gold, it tends to stop moving under conditions very similar to those that affect gold. If any gold is mixed in with the black sand, you'll see it. Most panners dump both the sand and the gold into a small bottle and separate them later. The easiest way to separate them is to spread the sand and gold on a piece of paper and put them out in the sun to dry. When they have been thoroughly dried, a permanent magnet wrapped in plastic can be used to lift off the magnetite. The plastic keeps the magnetite from sticking directly to the magnet—pull the plastic loose and the black sand falls away. Other impurities can usually be carefully blown away from the gold flakes.

For light prospecting you can use an army-type entrenching shovel and a geologist's pick. If an area proves to be worthwhile, a long-handled round-point shovel and a heavy pickax may come in handy. Later on you can get into larger equipment, which costs more money and requires more manpower, but will handle a lot more material. You will also become involved with various federal, state, and county laws and regulations regarding mining. For serious prospecting you'll need to do more reading— there are a number of good source books listed at the end of this chapter.

Can you earn money panning for gold? Probably not. But then not too many miners made much money during the California Gold Rush. The whole thing was more a grand adventure than anything else. If you consider your gold panning as an adventure, it may not make you wealthy, but it certainly will be rewarding!

Okay, here are your basic sources of information on gold prospecting and mining:

How & Where to Pan Gold, Wayne Winters, $2.50

Where to Prospect in the Fifty States, Hayes, $2.50

Prospecting for Gemstones & Minerals, John Sinkankas, $4.95

Gold Fever, DeLorenzo, $1.95

Week-End Gold Miner, A. H. Ryan, $1.50

Gold Diggers' Atlas, Robert N. Johnson, $2.50

Let's Go Prospecting, Edward Arthur, $3.95

For another $1.05 you can buy the Department of Interior's "How to Mine and Prospect for Placer Gold," published in 1971 by the U.S. Bureau of Mines. This can be ordered by writing to: Superintendent of Documents, U.S. Government Printing Office, Washington, D.C. 20402. For a free catalog of mining equipment, definitely write to: Keene Engineering, 9330 Corbin Avenue, Northridge, California 91324.

There are several excellent, reasonable, up-to-date books on prospecting for gold. If you can't find them at your local bookstore or rock shop, check the catalogs of suppliers such as Grieger's and Zymex listed in Chapter 9.

• 7 •

Where to Look
in the Fifty States

Given the great geological diversity of the United States, you would expect to find a wide variety of minerals for the rockhound to collect, and you would be right. Indeed, there is only one state that hasn't reported mineral findings. Can you guess which one it is? If you can't you'll find out at the end of this chapter.

In this chapter the writeups for each state are awfully short—only the barest skeleton. Most states have dozens, hundreds, or even thousands of gem and mineral locations. For the better-endowed states you will need to purchase one of the regional guidebooks listed in Chapter 9. I've listed fifteen of these, but there are even more booklets and brochures put out by local rockhounds and clubs. You'll have to check rock shops for them.

The rockhound and lapidary magazines, also listed in the last chapter, announce many field trips to both well-known and previously unknown collecting sites. Try to join a local rockhound club, since the members often know about sites on private property, or locations that have never been publicized.

The following is a brief summary of what you can expect in each state.

ALABAMA has mostly sedimentary rock, with some coal and iron mined in the northern half. There is a wedge of metamorphic rock in east-central Alabama which contains good mineral specimens, such as yellow beryl and aquamarine.

ALASKA is physically and geologically complex, and still offers many opportunities for gold exploration and prospecting. The difficulties include vast distances, frozen ground, and harsh winters.

ARIZONA has two distinct settings—the high Colorado Plateau in the northern third of the state, and the lower desert south of the Mogollon Rim drop-off. Agate and petrified wood are fairly common, as are obsidian and Apache tears. Copper is the major commercial mining product, and many related minerals are also mined: azurite, chrysocolla, turquoise. A particularly beautiful and unusual stone mined in Arizona is fire agate.

ARKANSAS consists of plateaus of sedimentary rock in the north and west; these are underlain with crystalline rock in Hot Springs and Pike counties. Quartz crystals are common, but the most unusual minerals found in Arkansas are the diamonds in peridotite at Murfreesboro.

CALIFORNIA is grandly represented in minerals as it is in so many things. In the northern part of the state, and in the regions lying to the east and south of the Sierra Nevada, volcanic action has produced vast obsidian flows and the fire opals in basalt of the Red Rock River Canyon area. The Sierra Nevada, a great westward-tilted granite fault block, has yielded placer and lode gold, garnets, occasional placer diamonds, and tungsten in the form of scheelite. The arid southern part of the state is dotted with abandoned and working mines and mining towns. Agate is widespread. In the mountains east of San Diego, on both sides of the U.S.-Mexican border, there are lithium-rich pegmatites—an extremely coarse-grained igneous rock—which have been mined for gem-quality tourmaline and beryl.

A young prospector sorts gravel in search of diamonds at Crater of Diamonds State Park near Murfreesboro, Arkansas. These rare gemstones have been found in several states, but always associated with placer deposits.

COLORADO is a state of great physical and geological contrasts, with the high plains to the east, the Rockies down the middle, and mesas and plateaus to the west. The major mining areas and mineral-collecting areas are in the Rockies, where igneous rock has pushed up into earlier sedimentary rock. Gold and silver have long been important minerals in Colorado, but a tremendous selection of other minerals can be found in the state. Among the easier to collect are agate, carnelian, petrified wood, smoky quartz crystals, beryl, amazonite, and amethyst.

CONNECTICUT has a central valley with volcanic trap rock containing agate and jasper. The crystalline rocks of the mountains in the east and west contain a wide variety of gem minerals; the most noted are the tourmaline and beryl found southeast of Portland.

FLORIDA is underlain with limestone and lacks the igneous intrusions into these rocks which produce interesting minerals. Agatized coral at several locations is about as close as Florida can come to having true minerals, but coral and seashells can be used to make interesting jewelry, and should not be overlooked by the rockhound and lapidary.

GEORGIA has rocks of almost every geological age, from the newer sediments of the coastal plains, through the crystalline rocks of the piedmont plateau and the northeastern highlands, to the ancient folded and eroded sedimentary rock in the northwest. Most of the state's wide list of minerals is associated with the crystalline rock areas.

HAWAII is a series of volcano tops that protrude above sea level from great depths. Hawaii probably formed as the huge Pacific Plate moved slowly northward over a hot spot or plume beneath the Plate. Coral and seashells are your best bet here.

IDAHO has a wide range of geological features, making it an excellent place for mineral prospecting. There are rugged mountains and basalt plateaus. The Clearwater and Salmon river drainages have been little searched. The most desirable minerals are undoubtedly the fire opals of the Spenser area.

ILLINOIS is made up mostly of relatively flat sedimentary rocks, but a wide variety of jasper and agate nodules have been formed, or shoved south by the glaciers. Lead, zinc, and fluorite are mined in the northwest corner of the state.

INDIANA is much like Illinois, with flat sedimentary beds containing fossils, but few collectible minerals. Gold and diamonds have been found in bedrock placers, as well as garnets, sapphires, and geodes.

IOWA has most of its collectibles in river gravels and glacial drift. Agate, petrified wood, and geodes can be found in Jackson County and at other locations.

KANSAS is basically high sloping plains formed by the sands and gravels eroded from the rising Rocky Mountains. Quartz minerals and agates can be found. Fossils from Kansas shales are well known.

KENTUCKY can be quite rugged, and was unglaciated. Jasper and agate can be collected in Ohio River gravels, and in gravel pits elsewhere. Garnets are found in Elliott County.

LOUISIANA is largely an area of flood plains made up of the fine sediments deposited by the Mississippi River. Thus it is not too rich in collectible minerals. Gravels of streams coming into the Mississippi from the east and the west may contain agate and petrified wood.

MAINE was stripped of layered sedimentary rocks by the glaciers, and large areas of crystalline bedrock were exposed. The most recent noteworthy discovery was made a couple of years ago when huge tourmaline crystals were found at Newry. Other mineral findings include beryl, aquamarine, and smoky quartz, as well as many of the minerals—feldspars, micas, quartz—associated with coarse-grained pegmatites.

MARYLAND's major area of interest (for us) is the Piedmont Plateau, west of the coastal plains. This area contains tourmaline, amethyst, quartz crystals, and lots of serpentine.

MASSACHUSETTS has most of its interesting collectibles in the area along the Connecticut River valley and to the immediate east of it. Here tourmaline, beryl, and other pegmatite minerals are found, as well as rhodonite, serpentine, agate, and jasper.

MICHIGAN's rugged and severely contorted igneous and metamorphic rocks to the north have produced both the rich copper and iron deposits and many of the specimen minerals associated with them—chrysocolla, datolite, epidote. One local oddity—and by definition not really a mineral—is Petoskey Stone, the fossil coral found on beaches and in quarries near Petoskey and Charlevoix.

MINNESOTA has its best mineral country in the Mesabi iron range in the northeast, where binghamite (a silicified iron), agate, and jasper are found, and in the Cuyuna Range in the central area. Beach and river gravels can contain good specimens of agate.

MISSISSIPPI is much like Louisiana—built almost entirely of Mississippi River sediments—only more so. Agate and petrified wood found in stream and river gravels are the only important collectibles here.

MISSOURI has the Ozark Highlands, which expose both sedimentary beds and crystalline basement rocks. Beautiful quartz crystals are the prize here.

MONTANA is often called the Treasure State because great quantities of gold, silver, and copper have been mined from the Rocky Mountains in the west, and moss agate and other quartz minerals have been found in the eroded high plains in the east.

NEBRASKA is basically made up of high sloping plains. The eroded valleys, where agate, jasper, and petrified wood can be found, are the best bet for mineral hunting.

In Michigan the water and ice action along the lake shores produces a constantly renewed source of colorful minerals which
can be shaped or tumbled to make unusual jewelry or specimens.

NEVADA is called the Silver State because of the tremendous production from the mines at Virginia City toward the end of the last century. Fire opal is found in several places—notably, the Virgin Valley in the north, and near Gabbs in the west-central portion of the state. Turquoise of high quality is mined in several places, and agate, jasper, and obsidian Apache tears are widespread. One of the world's largest mineral show-swap-meet-tailgate fiestas is held at Quartzite every year on the first weekend in February.

NEW HAMPSHIRE has a wide variety of gemstones somewhat similar to those of Maine: beryl, amethyst, topaz, and other pegmatite minerals. Most of the minerals can be found in the White Mountains. A well-known fee location is the old Ruggles Mine in Grafton County.

NEW JERSEY is best known, mineralogically speaking, for the famous Franklin mines, near Franklin. The mines produced literally scores of lead and zinc minerals, many of which can only be found at this location. Agate, jasper, serpentine, and even nonmineral amber are also found in New Jersey.

NEW MEXICO is at the southern end of the great Rocky Mountain chain. The mountains and several other minor uplifts expose a wide variety of crystalline and metamorphic rocks. Along with the expected agates and petrified woods, there are sources of peridot, unakite, pyrope garnets, and flashy quartz crystals in gypsum called Pecos Diamonds. These are very similar in appearance and origin to the Herkimer Diamonds of New York State.

NEW YORK is made up of several mountain complexes, with exposures of granitic and other crystalline rocks dating from quite ancient to more recent times. There are pegmatite dikes and the minerals usually associated with them: tourmaline, beryl, chrysoberyl. There are also the famed Herkimer Diamonds, quartz crystals in Herkimer County, as well as quartz minerals, serpentine, and labradorite feldspar.

NORTH CAROLINA is mountainous in the west—beyond the Blue Ridge and into the Appalachians—and most of the collectibles are found in the crystalline and metamorphic rocks of this area. There are many excellent fee areas in North Carolina, and the gemstones and other minerals that can be found include unakite, ruby, aquamarine, golden beryl, amazonite (feldspar), sapphire, and emeralds. Few really large stones have been found—that is to say, none that would become the crown jewels of an emperor—but there are a lot of very nice small stones. Many are of quite superior quality and would do well for faceting.

NORTH DAKOTA, particularly in the eroded high plateau to the west and in the Badlands, offers petrified wood, moss agate, and other forms of fine-grained or cryptocrystalline quartz.

OHIO is underlain with tilted limestones, most of them scoured by the continental glaciers. No granites have welled up beneath the limestones to enrich them, but fossils are common. Flint, sometimes brightly colored, is the only important mineral in Ohio, and it is excellent for tumbling or chipping.

OKLAHOMA is, for the most part, an area of petrified wood and agates, despite its minor uplifts of the Ozarks and Arbuckle mountains, the Wichitas and the Chautauquas.

OREGON is one of the best states for the collector of agates, jaspers, and picture-rock jaspers. In the south-central and southeastern parts of the state there are literally dozens of prime fee areas, and open land areas where beautiful tumbling and cutting material can be collected. Prineville in Cook County has organized several of the key collecting areas into a tourist-rockhound package, offering campgrounds and lead-you-by-the-hand tours. Write to the state at the address listed in Chapter 9 for some very well done pamphlets.

PENNSYLVANIA has a wide variety of minerals, located mostly in the Piedmont Plateau and highlands. Here the basement rocks are crystalline, granitic, and/or volcanic. There are also sources of many of the quartz-family minerals, such as amethyst, and of the pegmatite minerals, including tourmaline and beryl.

RHODE ISLAND is, for the most part, a dissected coastal plain, with some of the sediments removed by the continental glaciers to expose crystalline bedrock. Many of the quartz minerals, agates, and jasper come from the sediments; serpentine is also collected.

SOUTH CAROLINA is made up largely of coastal plains. In the northwest, however, the Blue Ridge Mountains of the Appalachians form the same basic collecting area as they do in Georgia and North Carolina. There are petrified wood, quartz minerals such as amethyst, and gemstones including aquamarine, sapphire, beryl, and garnet.

SOUTH DAKOTA has most of its collectibles west of the Missouri River; agates and such are found in the eroded prairie country, gemstones in the pegmatites of the granitic Black Hills. Tourmaline, beryl, and lepidolite are mined from the pegmatite dikes.

TENNESSEE is underlain with sedimentary rocks, so the main collectible minerals here are agates, jaspers, and chalcedony.

TEXAS is basically composed of coastal sediments dipping into the Gulf of Mexico. A wide variety of agate and jasper is available. The crystalline Llano Uplift and the mountains of western Texas produce garnets, topaz, amazonite, and quartz crystals. Amber is found in Terlingua Creek.

UTAH contains relatively flat sedimentary beds, rich in fossils, agates, and jaspers, as well as rugged mountain uplifts such as the Uintas. The relatively rare mineral variscite, which makes beautiful cabochons, is found in Utah; most of the known variscite sources are located on private claims. Topaz crystals are found in rhyolite in Juab County. The Bureau of Land Management has preserved the famous Dugway geode collecting site for amateur rockhounds.

VERMONT is made up predominantly of the Green and Taconic mountains. Erosion and continental glaciation has left great areas of the underlying productive rocks exposed. Collectible here are cyanite, staurolite, serpentine, dolomitic marble, and idocrase.

VIRGINIA's Blue Ridge and Allegheny mountains contain many gem minerals, and the limestone caves of the sedimentary areas contain other specimens of interest. Quartz is found in several variations: amethyst, smoky, and agate. Unakite, a relatively rare rock composed of pink feldspar, green epidote, and white quartz, is available in numerous places. Garnet, amazonite feldspar, beryl, and rhodonite are also found.

WASHINGTON is somewhat similar to Oregon in that the flat sediments and volcanic beds in the eastern part of the state produce the most minerals and contain agate and petrified wood. Carnelian, a reddish-brown form of agate, usually unbanded, is found at many known locations.

WEST VIRGINIA does not produce abundant mineral specimens, although one would expect some agate in the western Allegheny Plateau valleys. Quartz crystals have been reported in Morgan County sand pits.

WISCONSIN is basically underlain with flat sedimentary beds, but these are often broken by uplifts of granitic and metamorphic rocks. Aside from the Lake Superior agate in the glacial gravels, very little has been found so far to interest the lapidary or rock hound. The Baraboo Hills and the granitic and gneissic intrusions could warrant prospecting.

WYOMING has both high plains and complex upthrusts of igneous rock, with contorted and faulted sedimentary beds. Agate and petrified wood are found in abundance in stream gravels. Nephrite jade, varying in color from light green through darker green to black, is found at quite a few locations.

Did you spot the state with no minerals? It's Delaware, an area composed entirely of flat coastal plains, with no outcroppings of crystalline rock or highly folded and contorted sediments.

· 8 ·

Sixty Common Minerals and How to Tell Them Apart

If you have ever looked at a large mineral collection at a gem show or at a museum, you may have thought, "I'm never going to be able to remember all those different rocks!" And you probably won't be able to; but take heart—neither can most geologists or mineralogists.

Somewhere between two thousand and twenty-five hundred separate minerals have been officially identified, and new ones get added to the list every year. But —and it's an important "but"—there are only sixty at the most that you will come across in the field with any regularity. If you have a pretty good idea of what these sixty look like, you're way ahead of the game.

Minerals are identified by the various characteristics they possess. Some of these characteristics are easy to spot, others are more difficult. In this chapter I will give you a system of identification which relies on the four most obvious characteristics: color, luster, streak, and hardness. Other systems, which might be necessary to

To make your collection more interesting, it is a nice touch to be able to label each specimen with its name and the location at which it was collected.

identify hard cases, are more at the laboratory level, and would include crystal form, specific gravity, and cleavage or fracture. I'll tell you a little bit about these, but you don't need to worry too much about them until your collection gets quite advanced, and you're into crystallography.

The most obvious characteristic that will identify most minerals is color. Many minerals have quite distinctive colors: the lilac color of lepidolite, the purple of amethyst quartz or fluorite, the blues and greens of the copper minerals. Others run through a wide range of colors; usually these are caused by minor impurities. The quartz minerals—agates, jaspers, and petrified woods—are spectacular examples of color deviations. But, for starters, color is an important key to a mineral's identity.

Luster, when combined with color and other characteristics, is frequently quite distinctive to a particular mineral. Is the luster metallic? Definitely so in many cases: pyrite, galena, pyrolusite. Other minerals are glassy or vitreous; some sparkle even more, like diamonds (called adamantine luster); others have a resinous look; some are silky. All of these surface appearances or lusters, when differentiated from color, are easy and excellent ways to identify mineral specimens.

The streak of a mineral is found by rubbing a piece of the unknown material across an unglazed floor tile. These tiles can be bought through mineral supply or building supply stores. The handiest size is a two-inch white hexagonal. Some minerals leave a very definite streak, often in a color quite different from the apparent color of the mineral itself. Iron pyrite is a light yellow brassy color, with a very metallic luster, yet its streak is deep black. Many minerals, the majority for that matter, do not give a colored streak. If they are harder than the unglazed tile, they will leave none. But even when they are softer, the streak may be colorless. This in itself is a characteristic that can be useful in distinguishing similar-appearing minerals.

Hardness is the fourth characteristic for identifying minerals and it is relatively easy to use. Hardness has been defined as a material's resistance to abrasion. In other words, one material is harder than another if it can scratch the other, but cannot be scratched by it. There are several systems of measuring and rating hardness, but the one most widely used in geology and mineralogy is the Mohs Hardness Scale, which was mentioned in Chapter 2. The scale runs from the softest mineral, talc, to the hardest, diamond, with talc as Mohs 1 and diamond as Mohs 10.

For our purposes in identifying minerals, we don't

Scratch plates are pieces of unglazed porcelain tile. Most minerals rubbed across the plate will leave a distinctive mark. Some minerals leave no mark, and this in itself can be a useful bit of evidence.

even have to worry about the fine points of the Mohs Scale numbers because most mineral guides classify the hardness of minerals in four neat categories: softer than 2½, between 2½ and 5½, between 5½ and 7, and harder than 7. You may wonder why this strange division should be made. There is a practical explanation. Your fingernails have a hardness of Mohs 2½. Therefore any mineral specimen you can scratch with your fingernail is softer than 2½. The blade of the average pocketknife has a hardness of 5½, and quartz, a very common mineral, has a hardness of 7.

If you are collecting minerals for lapidary work—to polish them to gemstones of one type or another—you could say that anything your pocketknife could not scratch would probably be satisfactory, and those minerals that you couldn't scratch with a fragment of quartz would be even better.

The next test for mineral identification, and more complicated than those that we will use in this chapter, is specific gravity. To determine specific gravity—and it can be a critical factor in difficult cases—you need special scales that allow you to weigh a mineral specimen in and out of water. This can be messy. And an additional problem is that the specimen must be a pure sample of the mineral you want to check; it must be without contamination or adulteration.

Cleavage and fracture of individual minerals—the way they naturally break—can be an identifying characteristic, but in most field specimens, these features are apt to be rather vague. Cleavage and fracture, though only mentioned in a few cases, are probably next in importance after the four clues I'll be using at the end of the chapter for setting up identity cards.

The final clue to a mineral's identity is its crystal form. In many field specimens the crystals are so small that there is no way to determine their form without a special microscope. Even the geologist's standard 10-power hand lens only shows a confused granular mass. These crystal forms are essential—indeed they are at the very heart of any definition of what is a mineral and what is not—but for our purposes the forms can be given scant attention.

All minerals, with the exception of a few amorphous ones such as volcanic glass, have one of six basic crystal forms. The different forms are related to the number and placement of the natural crystal faces—this relationship is too complicated to warrant further discussion here. These six crystal forms are called, somewhat in order of increasing complexity, isometric, hexagonal, tetragonal, orthorhombic, monoclinic, and triclinic. This is all you need to know for rock collecting. A more than enjoyable account of crystal formation can be found in any good textbook on mineralogy.

To set up your mineral identifier you will need a package of 3 × 5-inch file cards and a hand punch. As you can see from the photos, you'll need to make four holes along one end of the cards for the four divisions of the Mohs Hardness Scale. Another edge needs two holes for metallic and nonmetallic lusters, and two holes for colored or noncolored streak. At the bottom there are ten holes for the major mineral colors. This leaves one end of the cards open. I've used this end to punch two sets of two holes for extra use. You could use one set for good or poor cleavage and fracture. You could use it to show have's and have not's in your own mineral collection, or to indicate whether or not the particular mineral is found in your home state.

Now your job is to copy the basic mineral information from this chapter onto the cards. Use one card for each mineral. There are sixty sets of data here; fifty-nine minerals and two variations of hematite are covered. These are the sixty minerals that you are most likely to come across in the field. Gold, turquoise, and diamond are not included—they are desirable, but they are not common.

One advantage of this simple mineral identifier is that by the time you have finished copying the information onto the sixty cards, you will have retained a great deal of the information, thereby making identification easier even without the use of the cards.

If you do need the cards, however, use them this way: test the mineral specimen for hardness, using your fingernail, pocketknife, or a piece of quartz. You have cut the individual mineral cards so that the appropriate hole

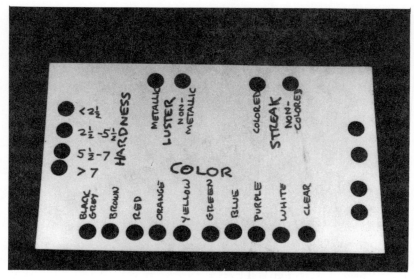

The master card of our identification set (above) has punched holes for Hardness, Luster, Streak, and Color. Extra holes can be used for additional information, such as occurrence within your home state. Each card is individually slotted (below) so that it will fall loose from the pack when a pencil or wire is run through the hole of a given characteristic. Each time, the dropped pile will get smaller, narrowing the mineral's identity.

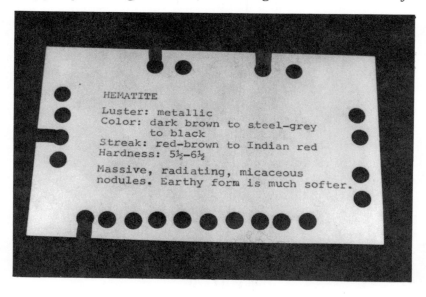

for each characteristic is now an open slot. If, for example, you insert a nail or piece of heavy wire into the hole for mineral hardness 5½-7, and jiggle the cards, only the cards for minerals in this hardness range will fall to the table. Put the rest of the stack aside; you have eliminated all the harder and softer minerals.

The same procedure is followed for the next most obvious characteristic. Let's say your specimen definitely has a metallic luster. Put the rod through the metallic hole and give a twitch—now the cards on the table are all metallic luster and 5½-7 hardness minerals. Streak and color are identified the same way. By the time you have tested three of the four characteristics, you should be down to a very few cards, and you may be able to figure out which mineral you have from other information written on the cards. In some cases there simply isn't enough information on the cards to eliminate two or even three possible identifications. In this case you will have to check some mineral textbooks, and perhaps a few more tests are required: specific gravity, chemical analysis, microscopic examination. If identification starts to get this complex, however, it may be simpler to toss the specimen out and forget about it. Or take it to the museum the next time you visit its mineral collection, and consult one of the mineral curators. It's kind of fun to track an elusive mineral and finally come up with its true name and composition.

The information given here for your punch cards is in alphabetical order. But it makes absolutely no difference what order you keep your cards in. The nail or rod will pull the ones you don't need out of the deck, and shower the ones you may want onto the table or floor. Keeping your cards in alphabetical order may make it easier to locate a particular mineral's card by name. This would be the only advantage.

AMPHIBOLE GROUP
Luster: nonmetallic, glassy-fibrous
Color: White, green, black
Streak: colorless
Hardness: 5-6
Crystals usually slender and fibrous. Group includes tremolite, actinolite, hornblende, arfvedsonite. Cleavage angles 60 or 120 degrees.

ANALCIME
Luster: nonmetallic, glassy
Color: colorless or white
Streak: colorless
Hardness: 5-5½
A zeolite mineral, found in cavities in igneous rocks. Trapezoid-shaped glassy crystals.

ANGLESITE
Luster: nonmetallic, powdery to adamantine
Color: colorless, white, gray, brown
Streak: colorless
Hardness: 3
An oxide of the lead sulfide galena. Usually massive; may occur in small tabular crystals.

APATITE
Luster: nonmetallic, glassy
Color: green, blue, violet, brown, colorless
Streak: colorless
Hardness: 9
Usually green with hexagonal crystals and pyramid terminations. Also occurs in massive form.

ARAGONITE
Luster: nonmetallic, granular to glassy
Color: colorless, white
Streak: colorless
Hardness: 3½-4
Often radiating thin crystals. Cleavage indistinct. Falls to powder in candle flame. Similar to calcite.

ARSENOPYRITE
Luster: metallic to submetallic
Color: silver to silver-white
Streak: black
Hardness: 5½-6
Well-formed crystals, grains, or masses.

AZURITE
Luster: nonmetallic, crystalline to fibrous
Color: intense azure-blue
Streak: light blue
Hardness: 3½-4
In very small crystals. May be fibrous, as in the alteration of malachite.

BARITE
Luster: nonmetallic, glassy to pearly
Color: colorless, white, blue, yellow, red
Streak: colorless
Hardness: 3-3½
Frequently as platy or tabular crystals. Often distinct cleavage faces. Its high specific gravity for a nonmetallic minerals distinguishes it from celestite.

BERYL
Luster: nonmetallic, glassy
Color: bluish-green, green, yellow, pink, colorless
Streak: colorless

Hardness: $7\frac{1}{2}$-8
Green variety is emerald. Hexagonal crystals and pyramid terminations rare. Crystals often large.

BIOTITE
Luster: nonmetallic
Color: dark brown, green to black
Streak: colorless
Hardness: $2\frac{1}{2}$-3
Perfect cleavage in one direction. Irregular foliated masses. Cleavage flakes elastic. A common mica.

BORAX
Luster: nonmetallic, crystalline
Color: colorless to white
Streak: colorless
Hardness: 2-$2\frac{1}{2}$
Crusts and prismatic crystals. Found in desert areas. Soluble in water. Splinter will fuse in candle flame.

BORNITE
Luster: metallic
Color: brownish-bronze when fresh, purple when tarnished
Streak: black
Hardness: 3
Usually massive. Associated with other copper minerals —chalcocite and chalcopyrite.

CALCITE
Luster: nonmetallic, granular to glassy
Color: colorless, white, varied
Streak: colorless
Hardness: 3
Crystals show many forms and colors. Limestone and marble are calcite. Clear crystals show double refraction.

CASSITERITE
Luster: nonmetallic
Color: brown to black
Streak: light brown
Hardness: 6-7
A major tin ore. Can occur as twinned crystals. Often massive and drab.

CELESTITE
Luster: nonmetallic, dull to glassy
Color: colorless, white, blue, red
Streak: colorless
Hardness: 3-3½
Similar to barite, but lower in specific gravity.

CERRUSITE
Luster: nonmetallic, granular to adamantine
Color: colorless, gray, white
Streak: colorless
Hardness: 3-3½
Lead carbonate; heavy feeling. Associated with galena. Splinter in candle flame produces globule of lead. Usually in granular masses or platy crystals.

CHALCOPYRITE
Luster: metallic
Color: brass yellow
Streak: black
Hardness: 3½-4
Usually massive, but may be crystalline. Associated with other copper minerals, and pyrite.

CHLORITE
Luster: nonmetallic
Color: various shades of green

Streak: colorless
Hardness: 2-2½
Perfect cleavage in one direction. Irregular foliated masses or compact masses of tiny scales. Thin sheet, flexible but not elastic.

CINNABAR
Luster: nonmetallic, diamondlike
Color: red to vermilion
Streak: bright red
Hardness: 2-2½
Usually occurs in massive or earthy form. Mercury ore.

COPPER
Luster: metallic to submetallic
Color: copper red, tarnishes black
Streak: shiny copper red
Hardness: 2½-3
Malleable. Twisted masses, irregular grains, branching crystal groups.

CORUNDUM
Luster: nonmetallic, glassy to diamond-bright
Color: colorless, gray, blue, red, yellow, brown, green
Streak: colorless
Hardness: 9
Includes rubies and sapphires. Crude barrel-shaped crystals.

CUPRITE
Luster: submetallic to metallic
Color: reddish-brown to deep red
Streak: reddish-brown to Indian red
Hardness: 3½-4
Ruby red if transparent. Massive or in cubes or octahedrons. Associated with other copper oxide minerals.

DOLOMITE
Luster: nonmetallic, granular to pearly
Color: colorless, white, pink
Streak: colorless
Hardness: 3½-4
Apt to be harder and more crystalline-looking than calcite. Occurs as dolomitic limestones and marbles.

EPIDOTE
Luster: nonmetallic, fibrous glassy
Color: yellow to blackish-green
Streak: colorless
Hardness: 6-7
Prismatic crystals striated parallel to length. In metamorphic rocks.

FLUORITE
Luster: nonmetallic, glassy
Color: colorless, white, violet, green, yellow
Streak: colorless
Hardness: 4
Usually violet or green, with distinct cubic crystals, often penetrating twins.

GALENA
Luster: metallic
Color: bluish-black to lead gray
Streak: gray-black
Hardness: 2½
Cubic crystals or cleavable masses. Lead ore. Very heavy.

GARNET
Luster: nonmetallic, glassy
Color: yellow, green, pink, brown to red
Streak: colorless

Hardness: 6½-7½
Usually spherical with many small crystal faces. Common in metamorphic rocks; also in igneous and pegmatites.

GOETHITE
Luster: submetallic to metallic
Color: dark brown to black
Streak: yellow-brown to yellow-ocher
Hardness: 5-5½
Occurs in radiating fibers, and rounded or stalactitic forms; rarely seen in crystals. Limonite form is more powdery.

GRAPHITE
Luster: metallic
Color: steel gray to iron black
Streak: black
Hardness: 1-1½
Greasy to the touch. Will mark paper. May be in hexagonal plates. Molybdenite's streak is greenish.

GYPSUM
Luster: nonmetallic, granular to glassy
Color: colorless, white, gray
Streak: colorless
Hardness: 2
Fingernail can scratch. Crystals and broad cleavage flakes. May be fibrous or compact. May look silky.

HALITE
Luster: nonmetallic, subglassy
Color: colorless, white, red, blue
Streak: colorless
Hardness: 2½

Common salt. Water soluble. Fractures in cubic crystals or granular masses. Salty to the taste.

HEMATITE
Luster: metallic
Color: dark brown to steel gray to black
Streak: red-brown to Indian red
Hardness: $5\frac{1}{2}$-$6\frac{1}{2}$
Massive, radiating, micaceous nodules. Earthy form is much softer.

HEMATITE
Luster: nonmetallic, earthy
Color: red to vermilion
Streak: red-brown
Hardness: 1+
Usually earthy. Frequently occurs as pigment in rocks. Crystalline form is metallic and harder.

HEMIMORPHITE
Luster: nonmetallic, dull to glassy
Color: colorless, white, pale green, blue
Streak: colorless
Hardness: $4\frac{1}{2}$-5
Often in radiating crystal groups or crusts. Also as smooth, almost greasy-looking rounded masses.

MAGNETITE
Luster: submetallic to metallic
Color: black
Streak: black
Hardness: 6
Major clue is that magnetite is strongly magnetic.

MALACHITE
Luster: nonmetallic, dull to velvety

Color: bright green
Streak: light green
Hardness: 3½-4
Appears in massive, radiating fibers or in rounded masses. Associated with copper minerals, particularly azurite. May alter to azurite.

MARCASITE
Luster: metallic to submetallic
Color: pale yellow to almost white
Streak: black
Hardness: 6-6½
Frequently shows up in radiating crystal groups or in radiating fibrous masses.

MOLYBDENITE
Luster: metallic
Color: blue-black
Streak: black to greenish-black
Hardness: 1-1½
Greasy to the touch. Micaceous; hexagonal-shaped leaves are possible. Greenish streak is characteristic; graphite's streak is black.

MUSCOVITE
Luster: nonmetallic
Color: pale brown, green, yellow, white
Streak: colorless
Hardness: 2-2½
Perfect cleavage in one direction. Most commonly occurring mica. Cleavage flakes are elastic.

NATROLITE
Luster: nonmetallic, silky-glassy
Color: colorless, white

Streak: colorless
Hardness: 5-5½
A zeolite mineral, found in cavities in igneous rocks. Often occurs as radiating groups of slender prismatic crystals.

OLIVINE
Luster: nonmetallic, granular-glassy
Color: olive- to grayish-green, brown
Streak: colorless
Hardness: 6½-7
Usually in small grains in basic igneous rock May occur in columnar masses.

OPAL
Luster: nonmetallic, dull to glassy
Color: colorless, white, yellow, red, brown, green, gray, blue
Streak: colorless
Hardness: 5-6
Conchoidal fracture. Precious or fire opal has internal plays of color.

ORTHOCLASE (FELDSPAR)
Luster: nonmetallic, dull to subglassy
Color: colorless, white, gray, cream, salmon, red, green
Streak: colorless
Hardness: 6
Common rock mineral. Often pink. Breaks into cleavage faces. Microcline is a variation.

PLAGIOCLASE (FELDSPAR)
Luster: nonmetallic, subglassy
Color: colorless, white, gray, bluish
Streak: colorless

Hardness: 6
Cleavable masses. Often beautiful plays of colors. Distinguished from orthoclase by fine, parallel striations (caused by albite twinning) on cleavage faces.

PYRITE
Luster: metallic
Color: pale brass yellow
Streak: black
Hardness: 6-6½
Often in cubes with parallel striations on faces, or in compact masses, or grains. The most commonly occurring iron sulfide.

PYROLUSITE
Luster: metallic
Color: iron black
Streak: black
Hardness: 1-2
Usually splintery or with radiating fibers. Can be used to mark paper.

PYROXENE GROUP
Luster: nonmetallic, dull to glassy
Color: white, green, black
Streak: colorless
Hardness: 5-6
Commonly found in dark igneous rocks. Differentiated from amphiboles by 90-degree crystal corners and cleavages. Group includes diopside, aegirite, augite.

PYRRHOTITE
Luster: metallic
Color: brownish-bronze
Streak: black
Hardness: 4

Small fragments are magnetic. Usually massive. Often associated with chalcopyrite and pyrite.

QUARTZ
Luster: nonmetallic, glassy
Color: colorless, white, smoky, violet
Streak: colorless
Hardness: 7
Often massive. Crystals usually have horizontal striations and terminal pyramids.

RUTILE
Luster: nonmetallic to resinous
Color: reddish-brown to black
Streak: light brown
Hardness: 6-6½
A titanium ore. In well-crystallized specimens there may be twinning and vertical striations.

SERPENTINE
Luster: nonmetallic, often silky
Color: olive- to blackish-green, yellow, green, white
Streak: colorless
Hardness: 2-5
Frequently appears as mottled green, and in large masses. Often a silky sheen. Appears as both a mineral and a rock. Chrysolite is the fibrous asbestos variety.

SIDERITE
Luster: nonmetallic, dull to resinous
Color: light to dark brown
Streak: colorless
Hardness: 3½-4
Becomes magnetic after heating in a candle flame.

SMITHSONITE
Luster: nonmetallic, slightly greasy
Color: brown, green, blue, pink, white
Streak: colorless
Hardness: 5
Occurs in rounded masses, similar to hemimorphite. Will fizz in warm hydrochloric acid; hemimorphite will not.

SPHALERITE
Luster: resinous
Color: dark brown to coal black
Streak: light to dark brown
Hardness: 3½-4
Usually found in grains or layered masses. Cleaves into flat, resinous surfaces. May be crystalline. Will always leave light streak.

STAUROLITE
Luster: nonmetallic, dull to subgreasy
Color: red-brown to brown-black
Streak: colorless
Hardness: 7-7½
Prismatic crystals, typically in cross-shaped penetration twins called fairy crosses. Found in schists (crystalline rock having a closely foliated structure).

STILBITE
Luster: nonmetallic, pearly
Color: white, yellow, brown, red
Streak: colorless
Hardness: 3½-4
Sheaflike crystal masses, flat tabular crystals.

SULFUR
Luster: nonmetallic, dull to glassy
Color: pale to bright yellow

Streak: pale yellow
Hardness: 1½-2½
Burns with blue flame and distinctive brimstone odor.
Heat of hand will make a mass of sulfur crackle. Granu-
lar, hardened flows; crystals.

TALC
Luster: nonmetallic, greasy
Color: white, apple-green, gray
Streak: colorless
Hardness: 1
Greasy to the touch. Can be micaceous. Hard to distin-
guish from pyrophyllite—only minor differences.

TOURMALINE
Luster: nonmetallic, glassy to subglassy
Color: colorless, red, green, brown, or black
Streak: colorless
Hardness: 7-7½
Slender crystals with triangular cross sections. Usually
found in pegmatites. Black schorl is most common form;
it is also found in granites.

ZIRCON
Luster: nonmetallic, glassy
Color: brown, red, gray, green, colorless
Streak: colorless
Hardness: 7½
Usually small prisms with pyramid terminations. Found
in igneous rocks.

• 9 •

Directories–
Where to Get Things

Where to Write for Information about Minerals and Rockhounding

ALABAMA Geological Survey
P.O. Drawer O
University, Alabama 35486

ALASKA Geological Survey
Dept. of Natural Resources
P.O. Box 80007
College, Alaska 99701

ARIZONA Dept. of Mineral Resources
Minerals Bldg., Fairgrounds
Phoenix, Arizona 85007

ARKANSAS Geological Commission
3815 W. Roosevelt Road
Little Rock, Arkansas 72204

CALIFORNIA Dept. of Conservation
1416 Ninth Street
Sacramento, California 95814

COLORADO Bureau of Mines
1845 Sherman Street
Denver, Colorado 80203

CONNECTICUT Geological Survey
"No information available."

DELAWARE Div. of Economic Development
45 The Green
Dover, Delaware 19901

FLORIDA Bureau of Geology
903 W. Tennessee Street
Tallahassee, Florida 32304

GEORGIA Dept. of Natural Resources
Earth & Water Division
19 Hunter Street SW
Atlanta, Georgia 30334

HAWAII Div. of Land Develop-
ment
P.O. Box 373
Honolulu, Hawaii 96809

IDAHO Div. of Tourism
Capitol Bldg., Room 108
Boise, Idaho 83720

ILLINOIS State Geological Sur-
vey
Natural Resources Bldg.
Urbana, Illinois 61801

INDIANA Dept. of Natural Resources
611 N. Walnut Grove
Bloomington, Indiana 47401

IOWA Geological Survey
123 N. Capitol Street
Iowa City, Iowa 52242

KANSAS Geological Survey
1930 Avenue "A," Campus West
University of Kansas
Lawrence, Kansas 66044

KENTUCKY Geological Survey
307 Mineral Industries Bldg.
University of Kentucky
Lexington, Kentucky 40506

LOUISIANA Geological Survey
Box G, University Station
Baton Rouge, Louisiana 70803

MAINE Bureau of Geology
Dept. of Conservation
State Office Bldg.
Augusta, Maine 04333

MARYLAND Geological Survey
Johns Hopkins University
Baltimore, Maryland 21218

MASSACHUSETTS Div. of
Mineral Resources
100 Cambridge Street
Boston, Massachusetts 02202

MICHIGAN Tourist Council
102 Commerce Center Bldg.
300 S. Capitol Avenue
Lansing, Michigan 48933

MINNESOTA Geological Sur-
vey
1633 Eustis Street
St. Paul, Minnesota 55108

MISSISSIPPI Geological Sur-
vey
P.O. Box 4915
Jackson, Mississippi 39216

MISSOURI Geological Survey
P.O. Box 250
Rolla, Missouri 65401

MONTANA Dept. of Highways
Travel Promotion Unit
Helena, Montana 59601

NEBRASKA Conservation & Survey Div.
University of Nebraska, Room 113
901 N. 17th Street
Lincoln, Nebraska 68508

NEVADA Bureau of Mines & Geology
University of Nevada
Reno, Nevada 89507

NEW HAMPSHIRE Div. of Economic Development
P.O. Box 856, State House Annex
Concord, New Hampshire 03301

NEW JERSEY State Geologist
P.O. Box 2809
Trenton, New Jersey 08625

NEW MEXICO Bureau of Mines
Campus Station
Socorro, New Mexico 87801

NEW YORK Geological Survey
Education Bldg. Annex, Room 973
Albany, New York 12234

NORTH CAROLINA Mineral Resources
P.O. Box 27687
Raleigh, North Carolina 26711

NORTH DAKOTA Geological Survey
900 East Blvd.
Bismarck, North Dakota 58501

OHIO Div. of Geological Survey
Fountain Square
Columbus, Ohio 43224

OKLAHOMA Geological Survey
University of Oklahoma
830 Van Vleet Oval, Room 163
Norman, Oklahoma 73069

OREGON State Highway Division
Travel Information Section
Salem, Oregon 97310

PENNSYLVANIA Geological Survey
Dept. of Environmental Resources
Harrisburg, Pennsylvania 17120

RHODE ISLAND Dept. of Economic Development
Tourist Promotion Division
One Weybosset Hill
Providence, Rhode Island 02903

SOUTH CAROLINA Dept. of Parks
1205 Pendleton Street
Columbus, South Carolina 29201

SOUTH DAKOTA Geological Survey
University of South Dakota
Vermillion, South Dakota 57069

TENNESSEE Div. of Geology
G-5 State Office Bldg.
Nashville, Tennessee 37219

TEXAS Bureau of Economic
Geology
University of Texas
University Station Box X
Austin, Texas 78712

UTAH Travel Council
Council Hall, Capitol Hill
Salt Lake City, Utah 84114

VERMONT Development
Agency
61 Elm Street
Montpelier, Vermont 05602

VIRGINIA Div. of Mineral Re-
sources
P.O. Box 3667
Charlottesville, Virginia 22903

WASHINGTON Dept. of Natu-
ral Resources
Geology & Earth Division
Olympia, Washington 98504

WEST VIRGINIA Geological
Survey
P.O. Box 897, White Hall
Morgantown, West Virginia
26505

WISCONSIN Geological Survey
1815 University Avenue
Madison, Wisconsin 53706

WYOMING Travel Commission
2320 Capitol Avenue
Cheyenne, Wyoming 82002

Mineral Museums in the United States

Here is a listing of the major institutional mineral collections. As you will notice, many of the collections are in col-
leges or universities. This frequently means that they are not
open to the public on a scheduled basis, but if you write to the
curator, telling him or her of your interest in seeing the collection, and when you plan to be in the area, he or she will
usually offer to open the collection up for you. The curator
may also be able to tell you about private collections in the vi-
cinity—these may be even more complete, particularly in specialized fields.

ALABAMA
University: Alabama Museum of Natural History

ALASKA
Juneau: State Museum, State Capitol

ARIZONA
Flagstaff: Museum of Northern Arizona
Holbrook: Petrified Forest National Monument Museum
Phoenix: Mineral Building, Fairgrounds Museum
Sedona: Meteorite Museum
Tombstone: Public Museum
Tucson: University of Arizona
   Earth Science Center, Sonora Desert Museum

ARKANSAS
Fayetteville: University of Arkansas Museum

CALIFORNIA
Berkeley: University of California Museum
Los Angeles: Exposition Park, County Museum
   Exposition Park, Museum of Science and
   Industry
   University of California Museum
   University of Southern California Museum
Oakland: Public Museum
Pasadena: California Institute of Technology
Riverside: Municipal Museum
San Diego: Balboa Park, Natural History Museum
San Francisco: Golden Gate Park, Academy of Science
   Museum
   16th and Roosevelt Way, Junior Museum
   Wells Fargo Bank Museum
Santa Barbara: Natural History Museum

COLORADO
Boulder: University of Colorado Museum
Colorado Springs: Colorado College Museum
Denver: Museum of Natural History
   State Museum
   State Capitol, Bureau of Mines
Golden: Colorado School of Mines

CONNECTICUT
Greenwich: Bruce Museum
Hartford: Trinity College
         Wadsworth Athenaeum
Middletown: Wesleyan University
New Haven: Yale University, Peabody Museum
Wallingford: Choate School

DELAWARE
Newark: University of Delaware, Robinson Hall

FLORIDA
De Land: John B. Stetson University
Gainesville: University of Florida
Tallahassee: Geological Survey Museum
         Florida State University

GEORGIA
Atlanta: State Museum

HAWAII
Honolulu: Bernice P. Bishop Museum

IDAHO
Boise: State Capitol Museum
Moscow: University of Idaho

ILLINOIS
Carbondale: Southern Illinois University
Chicago: Academy of Science
       Natural History Museum
Elmhurst: Lizzardo Museum of Lapidary Arts
Rock Island: Augustana College Museum
Springfield: State Museum
Urbana: University of Illinois, Natural History Museum

INDIANA
Bloomington: Indiana University Museum
Indianapolis: State Capitol, State Museum
Children's Museum
Lafayette: Purdue University Museum
Richmond: Earlham College Museum

IOWA
Cedar Falls: Iowa State Teachers College Museum
Davenport: Public Museum
Des Moines: Museum of State Historical Society

KANSAS
Atchison: St. Benedict's College
Baldwin: Baker University
Emporia: Kansas State Teachers College
Hays: Fort Hays Kansas State College
Lawrence: University of Kansas, Natural History Museum, Geology Department Museum
Ottawa: Ottawa University
Pittsburg: Kansas State Teachers College
Salina: Oakdale Park, Smoky Hills Historical Museum
Topeka: Memorial Building, State Historical Society
Wichita: Historical Museum Association

KENTUCKY
Lexington: University of Kentucky, Geology Department
Louisville: Public Library Museum

LOUISIANA
Baton Rouge: Louisiana State University, Geology Museum
New Orleans: Louisiana State Museum
Tulane University

MAINE
Augusta: State Museum
Lewiston: Bates College

Orono: University of Maine
Paris: Hamlin Memorial Hall
Portland: Natural History Society Museum

MARYLAND
Baltimore: Johns Hopkins University, Geology Department
        Natural History Society
        Academy of Science

MASSACHUSETTS
Amherst: Amherst College, Pratt Museum
Boston: Society of Natural History
      Jamaica Plain, Children's Museum
Cambridge: Harvard University, Mineralogical Museum
Northampton: Smith College
Salem: Peabody Museum
South Hadley: Mount Holyoke College
Springfield: Museum of Natural History
Williamstown: Williams College
Worcester: Clark University
        Natural History Museum

MICHIGAN
Alma: Alma College
Ann Arbor: University of Michigan, Mineralogical Museum
Battle Creek: Kingman Museum
Bloomfield Hills: Cranbrook Institute of Science
Copper Harbor: Fort Wilkins State Park Museum
Detroit: City Museum
      Wayne State University
East Lansing: Michigan State University Museum
        State Historical Museum
Grand Rapids: City Museum
Houghton: College of Mining and Technology
Kalamazoo: Public Museum
Marquette: North Michigan College

MINNESOTA
Minneapolis: Public Library, Science Museum
University of Minnesota, Museum of Natural History
Walker Art Center
St. Paul: Science Museum

MISSISSIPPI
State College: Mississippi State College
University: University of Mississippi

MISSOURI
Columbia: University of Missouri
Jefferson City: City Museum
Kansas City: City Museum
Rolla: School of Mines
St. Louis: Educational Museum of the Public Schools
Museum of Science & Natural History
Washington University
Webb City: Palmer Little Museum

MONTANA
Butte: Anaconda Employees' Club
School of Mines
Helena: Historical Museum
Missoula: State University

NEBRASKA
Lincoln: State Museum

NEVADA
Boulder City: Lake Mead Natural History Association
Carson City: State Museum
Reno: Mackay School of Mines Museum

NEW HAMPSHIRE
Durham: University of New Hampshire, Geology Department
Hanover: Dartmouth College, Wilson Museum
Keene: Natural History Museum

NEW JERSEY
Newark: Newark Mineralogical Society Museum
New Brunswick: Rutgers University, Geology Department
Paterson: New Jersey Mineralogical Society
Princeton: Princeton University, Geology Department
Trenton: State House Annex, State Museum

NEW MEXICO
Albuquerque: University of New Mexico
Santa Fe: Museum of New Mexico
Socorro: New Mexico Institute of Mining and Technology

NEW YORK
Albany: State Museum
Buffalo: Museum of Science
　　　　State University of N.Y. at Buffalo
Clinton: Hamilton College, Knox Museum
Hamilton: Colgate University, Museum of Natural History
Ithaca: Cornell University
New York: American Museum of Natural History
　　　　Columbia University, Geology & Mineralogy
　　　　Museum
Poughkeepsie: Vassar College
Rochester: Museum of Arts & Sciences
　　　　University of Rochester, Museum of Geology
Schenectady: Union College
Syracuse: Museum of Natural History
Troy: Rensselaer Polytechnic Institute

NORTH CAROLINA
Chapel Hill: University of North Carolina
Durham: Duke University
Raleigh: North Carolina State College
      State Museum
Spruce Pine: Museum of North Carolina Minerals

NORTH DAKOTA
Grand Forks: University of North Dakota

OHIO
Athens: Ohio University, Museum of Natural History
Bowling Green: Bowling Green State University
Cincinnati: Museum of Natural History
Cleveland: Case Institute of Technology
      Museum of Natural History
      Western Reserve University
Columbus: Ohio State University, Orton and Lords Hall
      State Museum
Coshocton: Johnson-Humrickhouse Memorial Museum
Norwalk: Firelands Historical Museum
Oberlin: Oberlin College
Oxford: Miami University
Springfield: Clark County Historical Society
Tiffin: Heidelberg College Science Hall
Toledo: Museum of Science

OKLAHOMA
Bartlesville: Woolaroc Museum
Norman: University of Oklahoma, Gould Hall
      University of Oklahoma, Stovall Museum
Tulsa: Fair Grounds, Science Building
      University of Tulsa

OREGON
Corvallis: Oregon State College
Eugene: University of Oregon

Portland: Lewis and Clark College
           Museum of Science and Industry
           State Department of Geology & Mineral Resources

PENNSYLVANIA
Bethlehem: Lehigh University
Bryn Mawr: Bryn Mawr College
Carlisle: Dickinson College
Easton: Lafayette College
Harrisburg: Geological Survey
Meadville: Allegheny College
Media: Delaware County Institute of Science
Philadelphia: Academy of Natural Science
               University of Pennsylvania
               Wagner Free Institute of Science
Pittsburgh: Carnegie Museum
University Park: Pennsylvania State University

RHODE ISLAND
Kingston: University of Rhode Island
Providence: Brown University, Rhode Island Hall
              Roger Williams Park Museum
Westerly: Public Library

SOUTH CAROLINA
Columbia: University of South Carolina

TENNESSEE
Knoxville: University of Tennessee, Geology Department
Nashville: State Division of Geology
          State Museum, War Memorial Building
          University of Tennessee, Geology Department
          Vanderbilt University, Geology Department

TEXAS
Austin: Texas Memorial Museum
El Paso: Centennial Museum

Houston: Natural History Museum
San Antonio: Witte Museum

UTAH
Salt Lake City: University of Utah, Geology Museum
               Westminster College
Vernal: Vernal State Park, Fieldhouse of Natural History

VERMONT
Burlington: University of Vermont, Fleming Museum
Montpelier: State Cabinet Building
St. Johnsbury: Fairbanks Museum

VIRGINIA
Blacksburg: Virginia Polytechnic Institute, Holden Hall
Charlottesville: University of Virginia, Brooks Museum
Lexington: Washington and Lee University
Richmond: State Museum

WASHINGTON
Olympia: State Capitol Museum
Spokane: Grace Campbell Memorial Public Museum
Tacoma: Washington State Historical Society
Wenatchee: North Central Washington Museum

WEST VIRGINIA
Huntington: Marshall College, Geology Museum
Morgantown: West Virginia University

WISCONSIN
Beloit: Beloit College
Madison: University of Wisconsin
Milwaukee: Downer College
               Public Museum

WYOMING
Cheyenne: State Museum
Laramie: University of Wyoming, Geology Building
Yellowstone National Park: Norris Museum

Mineral Dealers with Price Lists

Callahan's Gems & Minerals
P.O. Box 1006
South Pasadena, California
    91030

Dalton's Minerals
P.O. Box 17232
Tucson, Arizona 85731

Dr. David H. Garske
195 N. York Street
Elmhurst, Illinois 60125

Mathiasen Minerals
41149 St. Anthony Drive
Fremont, California 94538

McGregor & Watkins
Rt. 8, Box 487
Hot Springs, Arkansas 71901

Nature Arts Company
7136 E. Stetson Drive
Scottsdale, Arizona 85251

Orbetz' Showcase
Box 855
Kansas City, Missouri 64141

Reo N. Pickens, Jr.
610 N. Martin Avenue
Waukegan, Illinois 60085

Wright's Rock Shop
406 Airport Road, Hwy. 70W
Hot Springs, Arkansas 71901

Lapidary Equipment Manufacturers & Distributors

Alpha Faceting Supply
1225 Hollis Street
Bremerton, Washington 98310
    Send 65¢ for catalog.

Beacon Engineering Co.
Box 117
Rothsay, Minnesota 56570
    Free catalog.

Covington
Box 35
Redlands, California 92373
   Free catalog.

Crown Manufacturing Co.
910 Los Vallecitos Blvd.
San Marcos, California 92069
   Free catalog.

Crystalite Corporation
13449 Beach Avenue
Marina del Rey, California
   90291
   Free gem-cutting brochure.

Diamond Pacific Tool Corp.
25647 W. Main Street
Barstow, California 92311
   Free brochure.

Felker Operations, Dresser
   Industries
1900 S. Crenshaw Boulevard
Torrance, California 90509
   Free brochure on diamond
   saw blades.

Gemstone Equipment Mfg.
9330 Corbin Avenue
Northridge, California 91324
   Free brochure.

Gem-Tec Diamond Tool Co.
7310 Melrose Street
Buena Park, California 90620
   Free brochure.

Geo-Sonics
102 Lincoln Street
New London, Iowa 52645
   Free tumbling catalog.

Highland Park Mfg.
12600 Chadron Avenue
Hawthorne, California 90250
   Free catalog.

Hillquist
1545 NW 49th Street
Seattle, Washington 98107
   Free catalog on slab saws.

Hope Enterprises
6159 Columbus Avenue
Riverside, California 92504
   Free tumbler literature.

Lortone Division, Carborundum
   Corp.
2856 NW Market Street
Seattle, Washington 98107
   Free catalog.

Minnesota Lapidary Supply
524 N. Fifth Street
Minneapolis, Minnesota 55401
   Free catalog.

Raytech Industries
Stafford Industrial Park
Stafford Springs, Connecticut
   06076
   Free catalog.

TSI, Inc.
501 Elliott Ave. West
Seattle, Washington 98119
    Send $2.00 for general
    catalog.

Jewelry Supplies, Gems, and Minerals

Anozira Jewelers
P.O. Box 3988
Tucson, Arizona 85717
    Catalog $1.00, refunded on
    first purchase of $5.00 or
    more.

Goodnow Gems USA
5740 Canyon Drive
Amarillo, Texas 79109
    Free catalog of rough
    gemstone material.

Gordon's
P.O. Box 4073
Long Beach, California 90806
    Catalog of mountings $2.00,
    refunded on first $10.00
    order.

Grieger's, Inc.
900 S. Arroyo Parkway
Pasadena, California 91109
    Free catalog.

B. Jadow & Sons
53 West 23rd Street
New York, New York 10010
    Free catalog on jewelry
    making.

Silver Cloud Trading Co.
11833 E. Victory Blvd.
El Monte, California 91732
    Catalog $2.00, refunded on
    first order; silver castings.

Zymex
400 W. Los Vallecitos
San Marcos, California 92069
    Free catalog.

Books on Mineral Identification

These books may be purchased at bookstores or rock shops, or through the catalogs of suppliers such as Grieger's and Zymex, whose addresses are listed under Jewelry Supplies, Gems, & Minerals.

Textbook of Mineralogy, Edward S. Dana, $16.75.

Gems & Precious Stones of North America, Dr. George Frederick Kunz, $4.50.

A Field Guide to Rocks & Minerals, Frederick H. Pough, $4.50.

Gemstones of North America, Volume II, John Sinkankas, $30.00.

Minerals of the World, Charles A. Sorrell, $3.95.

Regional Rockhound Guides

These guides are available at bookstores or rock shops, or through the catalogs of Grieger's or Zymex.

Appalachian Mineral & Gem Trails, June Culp Zeitner, $3.95.

Arizona Rock Trails, Bitner, $2.00.

Gem Trails of Arizona, Bessie W. Simpson, $3.50.

California Gem Trails, Donald J. Henry, $3.00.

Rocks & Minerals of California, Vinson Brown et al., $4.95.

Colorado Gem Trails & Mineral Guide, Richard M. Pearl, $6.00.

Eastern Gem Trails, Oles, $2.00.

A Field Guide to the Gems & Minerals of Mexico, Paul W. Johnson, $2.00.

Midwest Gem Trails, June Culp Zeitner, $2.00.

Northwest Gem Fields & Ghost Town Atlas, Johnson, $2.00.

New Mexico Gem Trails, Bessie W. Simpson, $3.50.

The Rock Hound's Guide to New York State, Tervo, $5.50.

Gemstones of North America, Volume II, John Sinkankas, $30.00.

Gem Trails of Texas, Bessie W. Simpson, $3.50.

Western Gem Hunters Atlas, Scenic Guides, $3.00.

Rockhound Magazines

Gems and Minerals
P.O. Box 687
Mentone, California 92359
   $6.50 per year, 12 issues.

The Mineralogical Record
P.O. Box 783
Bowie, Maryland 20715
   $10.00 per year, 6 issues.

Lapidary Journal
P.O. Box 80937
San Diego, California 92138
   $6.95 per year, 12 issues.

Rock & Gem
16001 Ventura Blvd.
Encino, California 91436
   $9.00 per year, 12 issues.

Rockhound
3201 N. Frazier
Conroe, Texas 77301
   $4.50 per year, 6 issues.

Index

About the Author

W. R. C. Shedenhelm received his bachelor of science degree in geology from Columbia University, and did a postgraduate year at the University of California at Berkeley, where he was a teaching assistant in geology. He is chairman of the Backpacking Committee of the Los Angeles Chapter of the Sierra Club and Scouting Coordinator for an Explorer post active in rockhounding. He is also senior editor of *Rock & Gem* magazine.

552.075 Shedenhelm, W. R.
SHE   C.
C.2
            The young
            rockhound s
            handbook

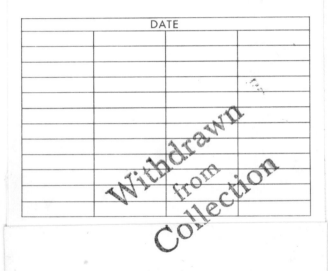

DATE		